Florence & Tuscany Travel Guide 2025

Robert Cox

Table of Contents

Chapter 8: The Ultimate Food & Wine Experience

Chapter 9: Where to Stay: The Most Charming

Chapter 10: Pratical Tips for Traveling in Florence

CHAPTER 1: WELCOME TO FLORENCE AND TUSCANY

1.1 Why Visit Florence and Tuscany?

Florence

Early morning light spills over the Arno River, painting its surface in amber and gold hues. The distant aroma of freshly baked cornetti from a secret café blends with the delicate scent of roasted coffee in the cold air. Footsteps echo in the nearly empty Piazza della Signoria, where the statue of David looms, perhaps watching over the city that gave rise to the Renaissance. Here in **Florence**, history, art, and emotion all combine to tell a story so gripping that every step feels like turning the pages of an epic novel.

Tuscany

 Beyond the bustling piazzas and renowned galleries of the city, **Tuscany** opens like a dream. Beyond the horizon, its rolling vineyards stretch, and historic villages rise out of the haze like timeless guardians of Italy's spirit. This is a location where life pauses to the rhythm of nature, where residents sip wine on sun-drenched terraces, leather craftsmen shape leather with hands that have been around for generations, and the wind brings the distant sound of an opera from a theater that has been around for centuries.

Why should you go, though? More than just a destination, Tuscany and Florence provide a journey into the heart of Italian culture, exploring the traditions, cuisines, and landscapes that have long inspired poets, painters, and lovers. Not just when you see Florence, you feel it in your soul. Instead than just experiencing Tuscany's story, you become a part of it.

Seeing Michelangelo's David or climbing the 463 steps of the Duomo to get a stunning perspective of the city's terracotta rooftops is only one aspect of a trip to Florence. An elderly Florentine woman who has been making pasta by hand for fifty years smiles as you try to order in Italian at a corner trattoria. It's about that quiet moment. It's about walking through an outdoor market in San Lorenzo while the aroma of aged pecorino cheese permeates the air and vendors announce their daily specials.

Outside the city walls, Tuscany has a certain kind of appeal. At a vineyard in Chianti, you might be served a glass of ruby-red Sangiovese by a winemaker who explains how the sun, the soil, and the traditional techniques give each drink its own distinct story. A nonna's laughter as she watches her grandchildren chase pigeons around the square and the distant ringing of church bells are the only sounds you might hear in a small medieval town like San Gimignano.

Florence and Tuscany appeal to those who are looking for beauty in the most fundamental forms, whether they be found in nature, art, or the most fundamental human relationships. However, to truly experience them, you must transcend the tourist's goal and embrace the spirit of this place as the locals do.

1.2 What Makes This Guide Unique: Beyond the Tourist Trail

When visiting Florence, most visitors bring a list that includes the Duomo, the Uffizi Gallery, and the Ponte Vecchio. To find the strange beauty mentioned in guidebooks, the usual itinerary is carefully followed—check, tick, tick—before boarding a train to the Tuscan countryside. But what if there was more to your journey than just visiting famous places? Imagine being able to move through the streets more like a local than a visitor.

By exploring the places, traditions, and relationships that make travel really unique, this guide offers a way to experience Florence and Tuscany beyond the tourist clichés. Instead of you simply enjoying the Gates of Paradise on Florence's Baptistery, you will hear the little-known story of how these golden panels were saved from destruction during World War II. You will know just when to visit the Uffizi Gallery (hint: weekday mornings) and which masterpieces to spend more time admiring without having to deal with the crowds.

You will visit places where Florence is still owned by the Florentines on this tour. Crossing the river, it takes you to the Oltrarno region, where craftspeople still work on gold and silver in their small workshops much as they did under the Medici. It guides you to buchette del vino, or secret wine doors, which are little openings in old walls where inhabitants have been trading a few bits for a cup of Chianti for decades.

Not all of Tuscany's treasures can be found along the popular roads. The owner will pour the wine and tell you about the property's history when you visit family-run vineyards that aren't included by the usual wine tours. You'll enter Pienza's hidden cheese caves, where pecorino wheels slowly deteriorate behind ancient stone walls, waiting for the perfect moment to be sliced and savored. You'll walk through abandoned monasteries where nature has slowly taken back the ruins, creating an eerie yet beautiful blend of the natural world and the past.

Since a journey isn't just about where you go but also how you experience it, this book is packed with advice on how to avoid tourist traps, navigate Florence's congested streets like a local, and locate secret spots where Tuscany's charm really shines.

1.3 Essential Travel Mindset: Living Like a Local in Florence and Tuscany

A slower, richer, and more traditional pace of life is what it's like to enter Tuscany and Florence. To truly experience this area, you must give up your tourist mindset and adopt a local way of life.

The first lesson? Slow down. You should not rush life, just like the Italians. A warm cornetto or flaky sfogliatella with an espresso, eaten at the counter of a traditional café, is a ritual breakfast that should not be rushed through. Sitting at a table will cost a little extra, maybe €2 to €5 more depending on where you go, but that's the price of absorbing the city's vitality.

Don't eat dinner at six o'clock. In Tuscany, dinner is a social occasion that begins at 8 p.m. at the latest, staying late into the evening to savor platters of freshly made pici pasta, bistecca alla Fiorentina, and endless glasses of wine. The best meals are found in small trattorias tucked away down quiet alleys where the chef's opinion is trusted and the specials of the day are posted on a chalkboard, not in restaurants with English menus.

Transportation? Although walking is the best way to see Florence, navigating Tuscany requires familiarity with the local bus and train systems, or even better, a rental car. The freedom to explore the stunning slopes of Val d'Orcia or discover an undiscovered village is priceless, even though a modest rental costs between €40 and €60 per day. Be prepared for winding roads and passionate Italian drivers, but embrace the adventure—it's all part of the charm.

When you visit historic buildings and places of worship, observe local customs. Several cathedrals, including Florence's Duomo, require modest attire that covers the shoulders and knees. The cost of admission can vary from €10 to €30, depending on whether you choose basic access or a full tour that includes the dome climb.

Perhaps the most important shift in viewpoint? Let rid of the expectation that everything must happen as planned. Examples of how Florence and Tuscany encourage spontaneity include the unplanned detour into a small town, the chance meeting with a local baker, or the decision to follow the aroma of roasted chestnuts instead of the strict itinerary you had in mind. These moments will shape your path.

CHAPTER 2: PLANNING YOUR JOURNEY THROUGH FLORENCE AND TUSCANY

2.1 Best Times to Visit for Every Experience

The sheer magnificence of Florence's Piazza del Duomo astounds you right away. The Renaissance's legacy is infused into every stone of the massive cathedral, which preserves centuries of history with its sky-high dome. However, your impression of this city will be greatly influenced by the time of your visit. The seasons influence not only the number of visitors, the pace of life, and the kind of magic you will find in Florence and Tuscany, but also your journey.

Slowly, the golden light of April comes into view. The cobblestone alleyways are not yet crowded with tourists, and the streets are still peaceful in the morning when you first arrive in April. The Boboli Gardens, where you may walk for €10 and see locals relaxing under centuries-old sculptures, are fragrant with wisteria. The days are pleasant and perfect for strolling along the Arno River at sunset, when the Ponte Vecchio is bathed in golden light, with highs of 18 to 22°C (64 to 72°F). Now is the perfect time to visit Florence and Tuscany if you want to enjoy the scenery without the incessant summer crowds.

Then summer comes, and Florence becomes a furnace due to the ruthless Tuscan heat. By July, the temperature has risen to between 30 and 35°C (86 and 95°F), and the heat is maintained by the stone streets, making daily walks exhausting. Tickets (€25 for standard admittance) must be reserved at least two weeks in advance due to the large number of guests. Locals travel to the coastal cities of Viareggio or Elba, while those who stay take refuge in gloomy wine cellars and sip Chianti Classico. If you visit during the summer, you may explore without being disturbed by the crowds and the heat, so early mornings and late nights are your best friends.

In the fall, Tuscany is painted in tones of gold and deep crimson. Chianti and Montalcino grapes sprang into harvest season around the end of September. Walking through these rolling landscapes leads you onto a family-run vineyard where you may sample wines straight from the barrel and pair them with slices of pecorino cheese for €20. The cool evenings in Florence, which average 15°C (59°F), take the place of the heat and are perfect for dining outside in Piazza Santo Spirito as the lights come on. If you're looking for a more upscale and relaxed experience, the fall is the ideal time of year to visit.

Then winter comes and Florence is once more the Florentines' domain. The streets are lit up with Christmas lights, the air is clear, and there isn't a long line to enter the Accademia Gallery (€16) for the first time. Saturnia's hot baths (€30 entry) offer respite from the cold in the countryside, with steam rising from the natural pools beneath the winter sky. Now is the time to go slowly and quietly, when you won't be distracted by big crowds and can savor every minute.

2.2 Packing Smart: What to Bring for Every Season

You realize as you take your bags out of the closet that packing for Florence and Tuscany is more than just packing clothing; it's about getting ready for a journey where every season calls for a different approach.

An wardrobe that can respond to various conditions is vital if you're traveling in the spring or fall. The mornings in early spring are chilly, about 10°C (50°F), but they warm up as the sun rises. A light jacket and a range of short and long-sleeved t-shirts are your best friends. Wearing comfortable shoes is recommended because the smooth stones of San Gimignano's medieval passageways can be difficult to navigate.

Summer is hard. You'll be sweating a lot by midday and will regret not packing an extra layer if you don't prepare. A airy linen shirt, a wide-brimmed hat, and sunglasses will make all the difference. When tourists underestimate the sun, they often end up waiting in line at a drugstore for after-sun cream (€8–€15) with their shoulders scorched from long treks in the scorching heat. Residents are aware that Florence's public fountains offer free, clean drinking water, which will save you money and keep you hydrated, even though a bottle of water costs €2.

Winter, on the other hand, is about staying warm and layering. At a café on Ponte Santa Trinita, a cappuccino costs €4.50 if you sit down, but €1.50 if you stand. The wind outside tears through your coat as you walk through the calm gardens of Pitti Palace, reminding you why it was worth packing a wool scarf and gloves.

Being prepared for Italian culture includes more than simply making sure your clothing are waterproof. Having a crossbody bag is essential for protection because pickpockets are widespread in crowded areas, especially near train stations. You may avoid racing to charge your phone in a dimly lit hotel lobby by investing in European plug adapters (€10). Above all, leave space in your backpack for souvenirs, as you will want to bring back bottles of Tuscan olive oil, artisan leather goods, and Montelupo pottery.

2.3 Getting Around: Public Transport, Walking Routes, and Scenic Drives

Although walking is the best way to see Florence, the experience doesn't stop at the cobblestone streets. The way you navigate the city and the Tuscan countryside shapes the experience, revealing the lesser-known sides of a place that existed before modern tourism.

On Piazza della Repubblica, where the soft hum of espresso machines blends with the distant ring of bicycle bells, you begin your morning. Because of its compact size, most of Florence's well-known attractions, such as the Duomo and the Ponte Vecchio, can be reached on foot in fifteen minutes. However, the streets speak for themselves, and if you want to experience Florence to the utmost, you must allow yourself to be separated from the tourists. In the

Oltrarno neighborhood across the river, people live their lives in small, quiet corners where little artisan shops still make gold jewelry and hand-stitched leather goods that haven't changed in decades. It's a short uphill walk to San Miniato al Monte, one of the city's most peaceful areas. The vast view stretches far beyond Florence's urban landscape, and monks continue to sing there in the nights.

Walking isn't always an option, though. The city's bus system, ATAF, becomes an essential ally, especially for traveling to places like Piazzale Michelangelo, where the sunset casts the city in tones of violet and gold. A single bus ticket costs €1.50 if purchased at a tabacchi shop and lasts for 90 minutes, allowing you to board and disembark as needed. If you buy the ticket on board, the price goes up to €2.50, which is a small but avoidable additional expense. Locals can easily navigate the city because they know exactly which bus to catch and when. Visitors must, however, adapt by looking up the schedule in advance and preparing for the occasional delay that comes with Italian transit.

 Beyond Florence, Tuscany lies in a region of rolling hills that begs to be explored. The rail, which offers direct links to Lucca, Pisa, and Siena, is the first point of access. The Leaning Tower in Pisa is a simple day trip that takes around an hour to get to and costs €10. The bus is usually a preferable option because Siena's train station is outside the historic center. For €12, you may go to the medieval wonder of Siena in 90 minutes.

But the countryside, where historic towns tucked away on hillsides meet olive trees and vineyards, is where Tuscany is most. When a field of sunflowers suddenly appears along the road or a family-run winery offers a €20 tasting of Chianti Riserva, the freedom of hiring a car totally transforms the experience. The roads themselves resemble sceneries from a Renaissance painting as they wind through the areas of Val d'Orcia and Chianti. A day's car rental typically costs between €40 and €60, depending on your schedule, plus extra for gas. The serene country roads outside of Florence's busy city center entice a slow, immersing excursion, despite the fact that some tourists are apprehensive because of Italy's unpredictable driving culture.

For those who would prefer not to drive, organized trips provide an alternative. Wine vacations to Brunello di Montalcino or the rolling hills of Montepulciano start at €100 per person and include transportation, tastings, and lunches in remote farmhouses where food is created as it has been for centuries. The logistical burden of traveling throughout Tuscany is eliminated by these carefully thought-out experiences, which allow you to savor every moment without thinking about parking or routes.

It becomes a part of the experience to return to your accommodation at night, when Florence's streets are less crowded. Although the last buses leave at midnight, it's typical to take a leisurely walk down the Arno in the late evening, when lamps sparkle on the river and the sound of an accordion from a distant piazza fills the air. Every stride, train ride, and winding road in Tuscany adds a new chapter to your journey, which is all about moving with purpose. It has nothing to do with speed or efficiency.

2.4 Budgeting for Your Trip: What to Budget for Accommodation, Dinning, and Attractions

The cost of traveling to Florence and Tuscany is a choice, not just a numerical calculation. Whether they choose the humility of a farmhouse surrounded by flowing vines or the grandeur of Renaissance hotels with views of the Arno, each visitor crafts their own interpretation of this experience.

 When you get to Florence, your first financial decision is where to stay. For €600 and above, upscale hotels like the St. Regis Florence offer evenings of unparalleled luxury, complete with breakfast served on private terraces and suites with chandelier-lit river views. For those seeking comfort without going overboard, boutique hotels and bed and breakfasts in the city's historic center, which range in price from €100 to €250 per night, offer the perfect balance. If money is limited, hostels are a wonderful choice because they offer dorm-style lodging for €30 to €50 per night and are occasionally packed with other travelers eager to share stories over a bottle of wine. You may also live like a local and buy fresh bread and prosciutto at local markets to prepare your own meals because Airbnbs provide entire apartments for as cheap as €80 per night.

Spending money on adventures and saving for essentials is the same strategy for dining in Florence and Tuscany. Breakfast is the simplest and least expensive meal, consisting of a fresh croissant and a cappuccino at a standing bar counter for €2–€3. Before disappearing into the morning hustle, locals swiftly finish their coffee. Lunch alternatives include a fast panino at All'Antico Vinaio (€5–€7), where you will be standing on the street with other hungry foodies, or a full-course trattoria meal for €20–€30, which includes a glass of house wine. In contrast, dinner is when meals continue into the night. The famous Florentine steak, bistecca alla Fiorentina, is best savored in pairs and costs at least €50 per dish. Away from the main piazzas, in quiet lanes, and across the river, San Frediano's restaurants often serve the same delicious meals at half the price.

In addition to meals and lodging, attractions can have an impact on the daily spending pattern. The price of admission to the Uffizi Gallery, which has Botticelli's "The Birth of Venus," is €25, while the Accademia Gallery, which has Michelangelo's David in all its sculptured splendor, is €16. The Duomo, its museums, and the magnificent Brunelleschi dome climb—well worth the 463 steps for the city view—are all accessible with combo passes, such as the PassePartout Ticket (€38). The Boboli Gardens (€10) offer a peaceful respite from the bustling streets with their secret fountains and Renaissance statues.

Transportation adds even more complexity to budgeting. Even though Florence may be explored without paying for transportation, moving outside of the city requires careful planning. While a one-way rail ticket to Siena costs €12, a full-day car rental for a trip through Tuscany's winding roads costs between €40 and €60, plus €15 to €20 for petrol. For guided trips, which include transportation, meals, and entry to unique locations, such as wine tastings or city excursions, budget between €80 and €150 per person.

When visiting Florence and Tuscany, the savvy traveler can use a number of strategies to balance cost and pleasure. It offers several free attractions, including walking through historic districts, visiting local markets, and watching the sunset from Piazzale Michelangelo. A rewarding journey without going over budget is made possible by combining free and paid events.

As the vacation draws to a close, the numbers vanish and you remember the days spent in galleries filled with timeless masterpieces, sun-drenched piazzas, and rolling vineyards. All that remains are the recollections—the sound of footsteps in a church that dates back hundreds of years, the laughter of an elderly Florentine merchant, and the scent of truffles following a Tuscan dinner. The purpose of coming here is not to spend a lot of money, but to completely immerse oneself in the friendly atmosphere.

Chapter 3: Must-See Attractions in Florence and Tuscany

3.1 The Grandeur of the Duomo and Brunelleschi's Masterpiece

Cattedrale di Santa Maria del Fiore

The **Cattedrale di Santa Maria del Fiore** in Florence is so magnificent that you automatically tilt your head back when you first see it. Its red-**tiled dome, white and green marble façade, and lofty bell campanile** all draw your attention skyward. It's more than just a cathedral; it's the focal point of Florence and an architectural wonder that draws admirers from all sides.

Piazza del Duomo

The throbbing sound of **Giotto's Bell Tower's** toll (€15 to the top) mingles with the sounds of visitors admiring the ornate carvings that encircle the cathedral's bronze doors across **Piazza del Duomo**. The Piazza, which was once the center of Florentine life, still has the energy of earlier times. Under the shadow of a structure that took **140 years to construct**, scholars, artists, and merchants used to gather here.

Baptistery of St. John

Before you enter, you pass the **Baptistery of St. John**, which is directly across from the Duomo and costs €10. Its golden doors—the "**Gates of Paradise**"—glint in the morning light. The biblical subjects in these panels, designed by **Lorenzo Ghiberti**, are so lifelike that Michelangelo himself thought they should be in heaven.

The cathedral's cool air greets you in stark contrast to the July heat outside. Despite its very simple appearance, the first thing you notice about the enormous interior is the dome above, which is **Brunelleschi's triumph**. Nothing compares to actually seeing it, even if you've heard and read about it. To get to one of Florence's most breathtaking panoramic views, you must ascend 463 steps to the peak (entry is €30 and includes entrance to the **Baptistery and Bell Tower**). Steep inclines and narrow corridors must be navigated during the climb.

Arno River

The city sprawls out below you in a perfect mosaic of terracotta houses and winding pathways, while the **Arno River** slices through the landscape like a silver ribbon as you reach the peak. At this point, you understand that Brunelleschi's dome is more than just a piece of architecture; it is a symbol of the Florence-specific human spirit, willpower, and inventiveness.

Opera del Duomo Museum

But the Duomo is not the only one who may enjoy the experience. The plaza has more hidden treasures to find. The **Opera del Duomo Museum** (€15 entry) offers a closer look at Florence's artistic legacy and is home to **Michelangelo's incomplete Pietà** and **Donatello's spooky wooden statue of Mary Magdalene**. Once a grain market, the neighboring **Orsanmichele Church** astonishes visitors with its Renaissance façade sculptures and Gothic splendor.

As you make your way back to the plaza, the **Duomo** remains your pivot, its majesty etched in your memory for all time.

3.2 The Uffizi Gallery: Botticelli, Leonardo, and Renaissance Legends

Uffizi Gallery

It's like walking into the heart of the Renaissance when you enter the **Uffizi Gallery** (regular entrance is €25, skip-the-line admission is €4). The corridors that stretch endlessly before you are lined with exquisite marble sculptures, some of the most treasured works of art in human history.

The first painting you see is **"The Birth of Venus" by Botticelli**, which depicts the goddess's ethereal beauty as she emerges from the water with its delicate lines and soft pastel hues. **"Primavera"** is a tapestry of legendary characters dancing beneath a magical woodland that grows next to it like a dream, and guests stand in awe of her immaculate golden hair and the way her position combines movement and calm.

"The Birth of Venus" by Botticelli

Leonardo da Vinci's "Annunciation"

Further down the corridors, you encounter **Leonardo da Vinci's "Annunciation"** in person. The young Virgin Mary is startled by the angel's word, and she is depicted so accurately that the folds in her garments appear almost real. This is where you may see the earliest signs of Leonardo's understanding of perspective and light, which would later revolutionize painting.

Raphael's "Madonna of the Goldfinch".

The way the mother and child interact in **Raphael's "Madonna of the Goldfinch"** is so delicate and charming that you momentarily forget you're looking at a picture rather than a window into a private moment, even though **Caravaggio's dark and moody chiaroscuro** conveys a sense of raw intensity and **Titian's bold**, dramatic brushstrokes transport you to the world of Venetian wealth as you move from room to room.

Along with the paintings, the gallery's architecture is a work of art, with the second-floor windows offering views of **Ponte Vecchio**, the **Arno River** shimmering in the afternoon light, and the city's iconic skyline. The hallways, which were originally designed to be offices for **Medici officials**, are home to some of the most valuable pieces of art in the world.

After hours of wandering this labyrinth of invention, the pulse of Florence's Renaissance still echoes in your mind as you emerge.

3.3 The Ponte Vecchio and the Timeless Charm of the Arno River

The weight of centuries of trade, ambition, and survival is evident in the bridge itself, which is flanked by small wooden shopfronts that seem to cling to its very edges. The Arno River, flowing leisurely beneath it, reflects the golden light of late afternoon, turning the scene into something out of a painting. When you cross **Ponte Vecchio**, you enter a realm where time is different and the echoes of old Florence blend with the present to create an enduring and enchanting atmosphere.

Ponte Vecchio

As soon as you enter **Ponte Vecchio**, you are drawn to the display cases of jewelers and goldsmiths, whose windows are glistening with handcrafted jewels. **Since 1593**, when **Duke Ferdinando I de' Medici** ordered that only jewelers and goldsmiths could sell their wares here, the bridge has been inhabited by these artisans, preserving an air of sophistication that persists to this day. The gold shines in the soft light, and the intricate pieces showcase centuries-old techniques that have been passed down through the generations. You witness a jeweler, his hands steady, polishing an exquisite gold bracelet that may have been worn by a Medici noblewoman centuries ago.

Halfway across the bridge, you pause to gaze at the **Arno River**, which runs on both sides and frames Florence's iconic cityscape, where the sun-kissed ochre facades of the houses form a graceful arc along the riverbanks, their reflections glittering in the water, and, despite the occasional removal by officials, couples lean on the stone railing and place miniature locks on the bridge, a new tradition that represents eternal love, while tourists, street musicians playing soft Italian music, and stores chatting with passersby fill the scene, their voices blending into the everyday harmony.

When the German army left Florence during **World War II**, **Ponte Vecchio** was the only bridge that survived. It is said that **Hitler personally ordered its preservation** because he believed it was too magnificent to destroy, but it stood as a shaky but stubborn tribute to Florence's tenacity when the nearby historic structures were attacked. This is something that many people are unaware of.

Few tourists know about the secret realm above the bridge: **Cosimo I de' Medici**, in **1565**, commissioned the **Vasari Corridor**, an enclosed walkway that connects **Palazzo Vecchio to Palazzo Pitti**, to give the Medici family a way to move secretly across the city. Although

36

currently closed for restoration, the corridor contains centuries' worth of secrets, including artwork, self-portraits by Renaissance painters, and the echo of Medici whispers.

Palazzo Vecchio

When you stand on **Ponte Vecchio**, you realize why it is more than just a bridge—it is a living, breathing part of Florence's soul. The bridge changes as the sun sets, the river is covered in shadows, and the gentle glow of lanterns flickers on the stone. The air is filled with the melodies of a violinist, which perfectly complement the river's rhythmic lap.

3.4 Michelangelo's David and the Galleria dell'Accademia

As soon as you walk into **Galleria dell'Accademia**, the excitement starts. You know what you are seeing. Everyone around you is drawn to the same piece of art, and their silent awe of the massive figure at the end of the hallway fills the air. Then, suddenly, there he is— **Michelangelo's David**, bathed in soft light, ruling the room like a timeless god.

Galleria dell'Accademia

David of earliar Renaissance versions

Standing more than **17 feet tall** and sculpted from a single block of **Carrara marble**, he is more than just a statue; he is a symbol of the strength Florence itself possesses, of human potential, and of defiance; every vein beneath his skin is visible, his muscles are taut with intensity, and his eyes are focused and determined; this is not the boyish **David of earliar Renaissance versions**, but a warrior at the height of his abilities, preparing for battle, his confidence unflinching.

As you move by him, you'll notice the delicate asymmetry that Michelangelo purposefully carved to give the impression of realistic motion. The fact that his right hand is a little bigger than anticipated illustrates the strength that God has bestowed upon him. His brow is creased, intensely focused, as though he is waiting for the right opportunity to confront Goliath. From every perspective, he is flawless—**a feat so remarkable that Michelangelo is reported to have muttered, "Why don't you speak?" after finishing it.**

Michelangelo's unfinished sculptures

However, **Galleria dell'Accademia** holds more treasures than **David**. As you walk down the corridor that leads to him, you pass **Michelangelo's unfinished sculptures**, known as the "Prisoners" or "Slaves," whose limbs jut out of the marble as though he had caught them in the act of birth, and who appear to be trying to escape the stone. The sculptor's belief that the role of the artist was to "**liberate the figure trapped inside the block**" is evident in their haunting, beautiful, and deeply emotional works.

Another room houses the **Museum of Musical Instruments**, a lesser-known gem that offers a glimpse into another facet of Renaissance ingenuity with its Stradivari violins and harpsichords from the Medici era that once filled the halls of Florence's magnificent palaces with music

You look at **David** one last time before you go, knowing that no photograph, no copy, no history lesson will ever truly convey what it is like to stand before him now, **Florence's eternal masterpiece, protector, and protector**.

3.5 Hidden Florence: The Secret Corridors of the Palazzo Vecchio's

As soon as you step inside **Palazzo Vecchio**, the history of Florence weighs heavily on you. The frescoed walls whisper tales of Medici power, political intrigue, and secret passageways that are only open to the city's elite. Palazzo Vecchio is more than just a palace; it is a stronghold, a symbol of power, and a labyrinth of mysteries just waiting to be discovered.

Palazzo Vecchio

Salone dei Cinquecento

The **Salone dei Cinquecento**, the palace's great hall, is the first thing that catches your eye. It is tall and spacious, with golden paintings of Florence's military victories by **Giorgio Vasari** on the ceiling. The **Duke's chair still stands**, as if waiting for Cosimo I de' Medici to return. But beneath the beauty lies mystery—there are recurring claims that an incomplete **Leonardo da Vinci** painting called **"The Battle of Anghiari"** is hidden behind Vasari's frescoes.

Studiolo of Francesco I

There is a network of secret passageways throughout the palace, from **Duke Gualtieri's chamber**, where a secret stairway hidden behind a fake wall leads to private rooms where Medici emperors used to hold secret meetings, to **Studiolo of Francesco I**, a windowless room filled with alchemical paintings, where you can walk into the head of a monarch who is fascinated by art, science, and mystery, where the air is filled with the smell of old wood and the gentle voices of guides whispering the secrets that were once whispered in these very rooms.

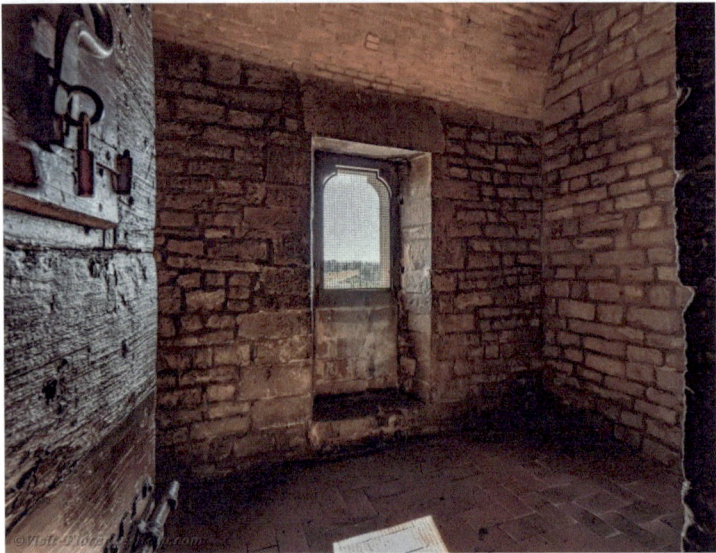

Prison of Savonarola

A darker section of the castle still houses the **Prison of Savonarola**, its small, cold room a memory of the religious fanatic who once plagued Florence before being hanged by stake in **Piazza della Signoria**, just outside.

As you leave **Palazzo Vecchio** and return to the golden light of the city's streets, you realize that Florence is about more than just the art and beauty on display in galleries; it's also about the secrets of history, the lost tunnels, and the stories hidden inside the stones.

CHAPTER 4: HIDDEN GEMS OF FLORENCE AND TUSCANY

4.1 Secret Rooftop Views & Hidden Gardens Florence

Piazzale Michelangelo

Away from the tourist-heavy streets, you'll find yourself navigating a little lane in the **Oltrarno district** and ascending a darkly lighted staircase to one of Florence's best-kept secrets: **La Terrazza at Hotel**

Continentale. The best way to see Florence is from above, where the skyline displays a tasteful fusion of ancient bell towers, antique domes, and terracotta roofs that reach into the Tuscan hills. While most tourists gather at **Piazzale Michelangelo**, there are other, lesser-known viewpoints that offer breathtaking views away from the crowds.

Unlike the busy Piazzale, you are surrounded by locals here, and the distant ring of church bells mingles with soft conversation. The rooftop bar, perched above the city, offers a comfortable setting where you can enjoy a **Negroni** (€15) while admiring the golden hues of the sunset painting the **Duomo's dome**. Below, the Arno River shimmers, its calm waters reflecting the flickering light of city lamps.

Torre di Arnolfo

The historic medieval tower, **Torre di Arnolfo in Palazzo Vecchio** (€12 entrance), is another unexplored sight that offers a close-up view of Florence's skyline. As you ascend the 418 steps, the sounds of the city fade away and are replaced by the echoes of history carved into the stone walls. From the summit, you can see **The Duomo, Palazzo Pitti**, and the rolling hills beyond, a view that was once reserved for the Medici emperors, who used it to survey their city.

Giardino Bardini

Beyond the roofs lie lush, private gardens that hold the secrets of Florence. In contrast to **Boboli Gardens**, where crowds wander the vast vistas, **Giardino Bardini** (€10 admission) is a quiet sanctuary in the **San Niccolò**

district where fountains gently flow into moss-covered basins and wisteria hangs over stone archways, offering quiet nooks where painters sit with sketchbooks and capture the subtle movement of light on old stone.

Giardino delle Rose

Another secret location further into the hills is **Giardino delle Rose**, a private garden beyond Piazzale Michelangelo, where over **400 varieties of roses bloom** and their scent fills the cool night air. As you sit on a bench and gaze out over the **Ponte Vecchio** and **Palazzo Vecchio** in the distance, you realize that Florence's true beauty is not just in its imposing churches and galleries but also in these peaceful retreats where the city whispers its secrets to those who seek them out.

49

4.2 Off the Beaten Path Villages Worth Visiting

San Gimignano

You follow a small sign leading to **Montemerano**, a village so small that it barely makes it on most travel plans, as you veer off the main road across the rolling countryside. Beyond **San Gimignano and Siena**, the real charm of Tuscany lies in the villages that have not been overrun by tourists. Tuscany is a region known for its ancient cities and timeless scenery.

Enjoy the tastes that have been refined over generations when you order a **plate of pici pasta with wild boar ragu** (€18) at **Trattoria da Caino**, a family-run restaurant famous for its classic Tuscan fare. The stone cottages are covered in **ivy** and have wooden shutters painted in gentle pastels. **Piazza del Castello** is a small area in the town center where it feels like time has stopped. People sit outside of small cafés and nod to you.

Piazza del Castello

Farther south, nestled between the hills, is **Sorano**, a town carved into tuff rock that looks like it belongs in an old fairy tale; its medieval walls whisper stories of Etruscan habitation, whose influence can still be heard in the underground passageways and ruins; explore its labyrinthine passageways to find **Orsini Fortress** (€5 admission), which offers expansive views of the valley.

Orsini Fortress

Castiglione di Garfagnana

Another diversion is **Castiglione di Garfagnana**, a fortress village nestled in the wild mountains of northern Tuscany, a wild and dramatic place, with a strong pine scent in the air, in contrast to Chianti's picture-perfect vineyards. It's a short walk up the historic walls of **Rocca**

Ariostesca (€6 admission), a medieval fortress, where you can look down at the meandering rivers that shape the valley.

These quiet corners and nooks, the unplanned stops in communities where the seasons, church bells, and the tradition of sharing wine at a communal table dictate daily life instead than tourist schedules, are what make Tuscany so alluring.

4.3 Underground Tunnels, Forgotten Churches, and Etruscan Mysteries

Most people are unaware of the world hidden beneath the streets of Florence and Tuscany, a labyrinth of tunnels, abandoned crypts, and ancient Etruscan secrets just waiting to be solved.

Oratorio della Misericordia is a simple church in the heart of Florence, and you descend a spiral staircase to find one of the city's best-preserved medieval crypts behind its altar, with its stone walls covered in faded **14th-century murals**. The air is damp and cold with the smell of history, and the flickering lights cast eerie shadows on the high ceilings.

Oratorio della Misericordia

Etruscan tombs and tunnels

The Volterra hills outside Florence hold a greater mystery: the town, once a powerful Etruscan fortress, now protects a network of underground **Etruscan tombs and tunnels** that predate the Roman Empire. The bronze sculpture **"Ombra della Sera"** at **Museo Etrusco Guarnacci** (€10 admission) is uncannily similar to a Giacometti figure, its elongated form frightening in its simplicity.

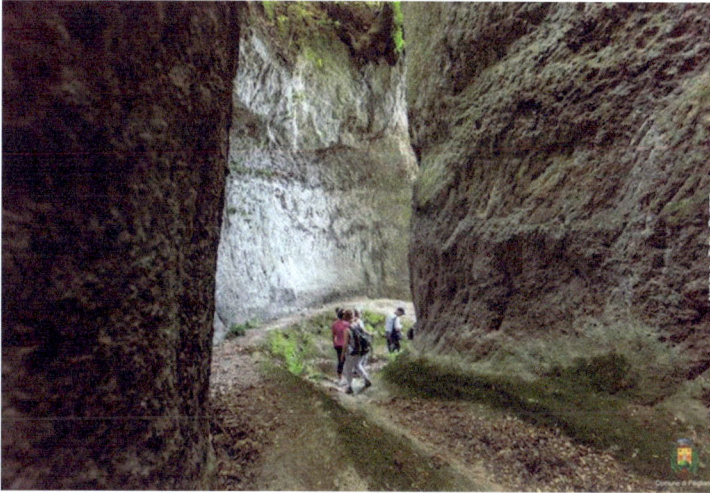

Vie Cave

Farther south, beneath the quiet streets of **Pitigliano**, lies the **Vie Cave**, an ancient labyrinth where Etruscan roads cut straight into the rock, with tall walls rising above you as you make your way through passageways carved over **2,500 years ago**. The size of these underground highways speaks of a civilization that once thrived here, its history etched into the very stone beneath your feet, and the silence is almost eerie.

Each journey into these underground worlds reveals aspects of history and stories that are simply waiting to be discovered by those who have the courage to delve deeper.

4.4 Hidden Wineries & Family-Owned Vineyards withNon-Tourists

Nothing compares to traveling through Tuscany's back roads, where the highways give way to winding lanes surrounded by tall **cypress trees**, their rich green contrast to the sun-drenched meadows; vineyards stretch as far as the eye can reach, with rows of grapevines winding up the gentle hillsides, their leaves shimmering in the golden sunshine; and, even though you are in the heart of Tuscan wine country, you are far from the well-traveled paths of the famous Chianti estates. **Family-run vineyards** here, in the isolated valleys and obscure farmsteads, preserve centuries-old traditions, their wines unadulterated by mass production, and their stories just waiting to be told.

When you pull up to **Podere Le Ripi**, a biodynamic vineyard in **Montalcino**, you notice a difference: no tour buses, no fancy tasting facilities, just stone farmhouses covered in vines, a wooden terrace overlooking the vineyards, and the heady aroma of aged oak barrels. The proprietor, Francesco, greets you with a warm smile, his hands smeared from the morning's work, and you follow him into the barrel aging chamber, where the scent of wine and wood fills the air, and the only sound in the silence is the faint echo of grapes ripening.

Podere Le Ripi

A **glass of Sangiovese** (€25 per bottle) swirls as he taps on a **barrique of Brunello di Montalcino**, the deep crimson liquid inside gradually maturing and becoming more complex, saying, "This is where patience matters." Unlike the large commercial wineries, each bottle here tells a different story, with each vintage influenced by the soil, the climate, and the hands that tend to the grapes.

Brunello di Montalcino

Val d'Orcia wine region

You find **Az** a short drive away in the less known **Val d'Orcia wine region**. I agree. The vines at the family-run **Il Palazzone** estate cascade down to a medieval stone farmhouse; the only sign welcoming anyone who happens to find their way there is a simple handwritten board at the gate; there are no signs pointing the way or an online booking system. Maria, the winemaker, pours a **Brunello Riserva** (€35 per tasting session) inside, and she talks passionately about how the wine is aged for five years before it is ever considered ready to drink. As the sun sets, the silhouette of the town of Pienza glows in the distance, and she implores you to join her on the terrace.

Bolgheri region

The **Bolgheri region** is more mysterious than Chianti and Montalcino, and few venture beyond the world-familiar estates of **Sassicaia and Ornellaia. Guado al Melo** is a small vineyard where history and experimentation coexist, tucked away on a quiet lane, where wine is made using only natural fermentation and maturing in terracotta amphorae, just like the ancient Etruscans did, without the use of pesticides or other artificial methods. The result is an unrivaled **Super Tuscan,** with the essence of the region in every sip.

As you stand on the edge of the vineyard and watch the sun cast long shadows across the grapes, you realize that wine in Tuscany is more than just a drink; it's about understanding, feeling the rhythm of the land, and connecting with the people whose families have been growing these hills for centuries.

Maremma region

A second kind of vineyard can be found further south in the **Maremma region**, where the sea breeze influences the grapes and gives the wines a unique minerality. The **Morellino di Scansano**, a wine from **Moris Farms**, a small estate near Scansano, is a wine that few outside of Italy truly like. The proprietor, an old man with grizzled hands and a loud, hearty laugh, pours **a glass of Morellino** (€18 a bottle), explaining how the **Tyrrhenian Sea** breezes contribute to its freshness. As you sit under a pergola with a dish of pecorino cheese and wild boar salami by your side, you realize that this moment—this perfect, pristine moment—is what **Tuscany** is all about.

Etruscan wine cellars of Montepulciano

Beyond the wineries, the historic **Etruscan wine cellars of Montepulciano** offer another glimpse into Tuscany's hidden wine culture: the **cantinas**, which are situated beneath the town's stone streets and have massive corridors lined with barrels that seem as old as the town itself, date back more than a thousand years. You descend a spiral staircase into the depths of history at **Cantina De' Ricci** (€20 for a tour and sampling), where the chilly air is filled with the scent of ripening grapes and seasoned wood, while the sommelier pours a **Vino Nobile di Montepulciano**, its deep red color shining in the darkness like a candle on a barrel. Here, you taste not just wine, but a thousand years of history.

Avignonesi

Before you leave, you stop by **Avignonesi**, a small vineyard between Montepulciano and Cortona, where the focus is not only on **Sangiovese** but also on Vin Santo, one of Tuscany's best dessert wines (€10 per tasting), rich, honey-like, golden, and with a deep, nutty character that counterbalances its sweetness after ten years of aging in small barrels. As you take a long drink, savoring every drop, the soft glow of dusk illuminates the endless Tuscan hills ahead.

Where winemakers pour their souls into each bottle, where stories are told over a simple supper at a wooden farmhouse table, and where vines grow wild in the quiet and obscure nooks, they may be discovered. Here, in these hidden vineyards, you become a part of the wine's story rather than just tasting it. The most memorable wine experiences in Tuscany are not found in the fancy tasting rooms of mass-market companies or the well-traveled Chianti itineraries.

4.5 Exploring Ancient Etruscan Towns & Hidden Monasteries

As stunning as its Renaissance towns and rolling vineyards, Tuscany's ancient past lies hidden behind layers of time, waiting to be unearthed. To truly appreciate this region, you must step outside your comfort zone and into the **Etruscan heartlands**, where villages perched atop volcanic cliffs tell stories of a civilization that predates even Rome.

Parco Archeologico Città del Tufo

As you drive toward **Sovana**, the landscape gradually changes as you approach a place untouched by the bustle of modern life: some of best-preserved **Etruscan tombs in Tuscany** may be found in this small medieval hamlet with few residents and no traffic signals; as you walk a narrow path into the woods at **Parco Archeologico Città del Tufo** (€5 admission), massive Etruscan burial sites carved into the rock rise all around you, broken only by the rustle of leaves and the occasional call of birds swoop overhead, and you realize that these abandoned remains are nonetheless alive with history as you stand in front of the **Tomba Ildebranda**, whose front oddly resembles a Greek temple.

Pitigliano

Pitigliano rises impressively from the nearby cliffs with its golden stone homes that blend in perfectly with the surroundings; its quiet lanes take you to the **Orsini Fortress** (€6 admission), where medieval history meets **Etruscan caverns** below; a secret passageway leads to the **Vie Cave**, a network of submerged pathways sculpted by the **Etruscans** over **2,500 years ago**; its tall walls enclose you in a dark, ancient world.

Time seems to have stopped as you stand in the courtyard at sunset, as the nightly chant begins, and you look out over the undulating hills that reach beyond the horizon. Monks stroll in peaceful reflection as candlelight flickers on the frescoed walls within **La Verna Monastery**, in the heart of the **Casentino Forests**, where dense forests and meandering paths give way to ancient remains. The air is chilly and has a subtle scent of moist stone and pine as you enter the gardens where **St. Francis of Assisi received his stigmata in 1224**.

Casentino Forests

A short walk leads to **Eremo di Montesiepi**, the location of the legendary **Sword in the Stone**, buried in the rock and the inspiration for Arthurian legends, a reminder of Tuscany's ancient mythology. Further south is **Abbazia di San Galgano**, another abbey, its Gothic walls without roofs standing resolutely against the sky, the sunlight streaming through the empty window arches creating an almost supernatural feeling. The monastery has been an open-air cathedral since the 18th century.

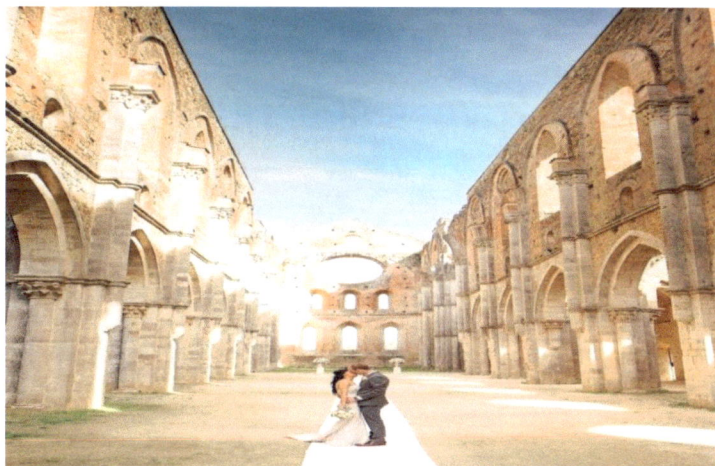

Abbazia di San Galgano

You discover that Tuscany is more than just what you see when you visit these sites; it's about what lies beneath the surface, in the ancient streets, the deserted tombs, and the revered monasteries that still guard their secrets.

CHAPTER 5: THE CULTURE FESTIVALS AND TRADITIONS OF TUSCANY

5.1 The Renaissance Legacy: Florence's Role in Shaping the World

The shadow of **Michelangelo's David**, which stands outside **Palazzo Vecchio** in **Piazza della Signoria,** reminds us that this is the beginning of the Renaissance, the period that irrevocably changed human philosophy, art, and science. Florence is more than just a city; it is a living museum and a work of art in and of itself, with each square, street, and building telling the story of the greatest cultural revival in history.

Standing beneath the massive **Brunelleschi Dome**, you realize how ingenious it was to build such a feat without scaffolding in the **15th century. Galileo, Botticelli, and Leonardo da Vinci**—men whose ideas changed the world—were born in this city, and the very streets you are walking on now were the scene of heated debates about philosophy, physics, and the human spirit.

68

Brunelleschi Dome

More than just works of art, the paintings at the **Galleria degli Uffizi** (€25 admission) are historical revolutions that bear witness to a time when human intellect was at its height, from the delicate brushstrokes of Botticelli's **"The Birth of Venus"** to **Leonardo's early works** and **Raphael's angelic portraits**.

At the nearby **Museo Galileo** (€10 entry), you hold your breath in front of the telescope that revealed the secrets of the cosmos, the instrument Galileo used to disbelieve the Church and rethink our role in the universe.

Museo Galileo

Opificio delle Pietre Dure

As you descend **Via dei Servi**, you enter Op**ificio delle Pietre Dure**, a workshop where Medici artisans once mastered the technique of inlaid stone mosaics, producing elaborate designs so minutely detailed that they resemble paintings. Florence's aura of artistic grandeur and intellectual defiance extends beyond the museums to areas that visitors often overlook.

San Miniato al Monte

In a stunning Renaissance vision, the city sprawls below, unchanged and unbroken, still speaking the heritage of the past to those who are willing to listen, while the Romanesque façade of **San Miniato al Monte**, one of

Florence's oldest churches, is illuminated by the last of the day's golden light as you stand there at sunset.

5.2 Tuscany's Festivities: From Palio di Siena to Wine Harvest Celebrations

Palio di Siena

The drums begin before you can see the motorcyclists, and as they reverberate through the medieval alleyways of **Siena**, their deep, repetitive pounding signals the beginning of something ancient and significant: the **Palio di Siena**, the world's most intense horse race, is about to begin in **Piazza del Campo**, and you are pushed forward with the crowd, the excitement growing with each step.

More than just a show, this has been a test of honor and a battle between neighborhoods **since 1633**. Each contrada, or ancient district of Siena, competes fiercely, with riders in medieval armor clutching the reins of bareback horses and their eyes focused on the dusty track where fortunes are won and lost in an instant. The sound of thousands of voices resonating off the centuries-old stone creates an electrifying atmosphere, and the feeling of being in the center of history is priceless. Tickets range from €50 for standing spaces to nearly €400 for balcony views.

Chianti Classico Wine Festival

The festive mood is different elsewhere in Tuscany, where at **Greve** in **Chianti's Chianti Classico Wine Festival** (tastings €10), the aroma of sun-warmed grapes and old wood fills the air as wine pours out of barrels, and local farmers with harvest-stained hands proudly explain how the land, soil, and seasons determine the vintage each year as they serve glasses of **ruby-red Chianti.**

Festa dell'Uva

Further south in the **Maremma region**, you are in the midst of **Scansano's** great wine harvest festival, called **Festa dell'Uva**, where people parade through the streets carrying baskets of grapes and the celebrations end with a never-ending feast, folk music, and dancing that lasts long into the night.

San Gimignano's Truffle Festival

By October, the penultimate autumnal celebration in Tuscany, **San Gimignano's Truffle Festival**, is under way, where the best delicacy in the world is hunted, auctioned, and devoured in a sensory frenzy that is sure to leave an impression.

5.3 Florence's Artisan Crafts: Goldsmithing, Leather, and Timeless Traditions

In **Florence's Oltrarno district**, where the streets are filled with the scent of freshly tanned leather, time seems to move more slowly as artisans continue to use their hands to transform raw materials into beautiful and functional objects, just as they did during the Medici era. Unlike the mass-produced trinkets that can be seen near the **Ponte Vecchio**, these works are highly personal and each bears the maker's signature.

Scuola del Cuoio

 Scuola del Cuoio is a leather school hidden **beneath Santa Croce Basilica**. In the soft light of the studio, expert hands painstakingly cut, sewed, and embossed gorgeous Italian leather into wallets, belts, and purses, and the earthy richness of freshly colored skins fills the air as the sound of hammers hammering rhythmically fills the room. Established to teach **World War II** orphaned

76

children a skill, this school is still going strong today, teaching centuries-old Florentine customs. Here, the artisans respect the material and take their time, allowing each item to develop naturally. Priced at €250, a handcrafted leather bag from this atelier is more than just a purchase—it's a lifetime investment that symbolizes Florence.

Fratelli Piccini

In a small goldsmith's shop on the **Ponte Vecchio**, across the river, an old craftsman leans over his workbench, a magnifying lens resting on his nose, and carefully shapes and twists a small piece of gold between his fingers. **Fratelli Piccini**, one of **Florence's oldest goldsmithing** businesses, has been hand-designing jewelry since the

Renaissance. Unlike modern manufacturing, there are no machines here, only tools that have been used for centuries, their edges worn smooth by time. **Duke Ferdinando I de' Medici** changed the **Ponte Vecchio**, once occupied by butchers and tanners, in **1593** by restricting the sale of goods on the bridge to goldsmiths, creating a refined atmosphere that has persisted to this day. A custom-made gold necklace based on Medici designs, starting at €500, is a piece of history that tells a tale as rich as the city itself.

Il Papiro

You are drawn inside a Florentine paper workshop farther down Via dei Serragli by the aroma of ink and ancient parchment. At **Il Papiro**, craftspeople engage in the age-old craft of creating marbled paper by dipping sheets into whirling colors to produce elaborate, one-of-a-kind designs. The colors settle into fine veins of blue, crimson, and gold, the same patterns that were previously used to bind volumes for the Medici library, and you watch as a sheet is removed. At about €35, a handcrafted diary with a cover prepared using these antiquated methods are the ideal memento—a blank canvas for your own tales.

In a culture that often undervalues handcrafted goods, Florence's artisans not only sell things but also preserve history, guaranteeing the survival of Renaissance crafts.

5.4 Opera, Music, and Theatrical Heritage: The Soul of Italian Performance

With its ornately frescoed roof and gold-leaf balcony, the theater's grandeur transports you back in time. After all, opera originated in Florence, where composers like **Jacopo Peri** experimented with music and theater in the late **16th century**, laying the groundwork for a form that would eventually take over Europe. The velvet curtains part as soon as you enter **Teatro della Pergola** (tickets range from €30 to €100), and the first chords of **Puccini's La Bohème** begin to play.

Teatro della Pergola

Teatro del Giglio

The song of Italy's most beloved opera composer still fills the streets of nearby **Lucca**, where **Giacomo Puccini** once lived. His arias are sung with the same passion as they were over a century ago in the tiny 19th-century **Teatro del Giglio** (€40 per seat). During the annual **Puccini Festival at Torre del Lago**, the city hosts grand performances of **Madama Butterfly, Tosca**, and **Turandot** at an outdoor theater by the lake where the composer used to live.

Volterra Teatro

But the love of theater in Tuscany is not just about opera; every summer, the medieval town of **Volterra** comes alive with **Volterra Teatro**, a festival that brings the medieval town to life with players dressed in Renaissance costumes performing **Shakespearean dramas in the**

historic Roman theater (€20 per performance). The combination of history, drama, and candlelight ruins creates an electrifying atmosphere that makes each performance feel like a window into a different era.

Accademia Musicale Chigiana

Set in a former Chigi family palace, **Accademia Musicale Chigiana in Siena** (€50 for an evening concert) offers some of Italy's best classical music performances, an immersive experience where the power of a single violin can hold an entire audience in breathless silence, and has trained world-class musicians.

There is also music in Florence's piazzas: street performers gather in **Piazza della Signoria** under the shade of **Palazzo Vecchio**, their violins and guitars blending with the sounds of the city; a lone tenor's performance of "**O Sole Mio**," echoing over the Arno at dusk, reminds us that music in Tuscany is more than just a show, it is the soul of the land.

5.5 Religious and Historical Events: Easter Celebrations, Medieval Fairs, and More

On Easter Sunday, there is a sense of anticipation as one stands in **Piazza del Duomo**, anticipating the **Scoppio del Carro**, also called the "**Explosion of the Cart**," which ignites a tall wooden cart with antique ornamentation in front of the **Cathedral of Santa Maria del Fiore.** A white dove-shaped rocket is suddenly launched from the altar and travels toward the cart along a wire, and if all goes as planned, it will set off a spectacular fireworks show, bringing Florence luck in the coming year. This tradition, which dates back to the **Crusades**, combines faith, history, and sheer grandeur to create an unparalleled spectacle.

Festa Medievale

In addition to its religious ceremonies, Tuscany is known for its **medieval fairs**, which turn entire villages into historical settings. **Monteriggioni**, a fortress town that seems to have been frozen in the thirteenth century, hosts the **Festa Medievale** (€10 entrance), which features minstrels playing lutes, blacksmiths forging weapons over open fires, and knights in dazzling armor parading through the streets. The street kiosks selling grilled meats, spiced wine, and artisan products give you the impression that you have traveled back in time.

Sagra del Tordo

The **Sagra del Tordo ("Feast of the Thrush")** takes place in the **Montalcino** vineyards further south in late October, where locals, dressed in medieval garb, compete for the honor of their region in medieval-style archery contests, culminating in a sumptuous feast featuring truffles, wild animals, and barrels of **Brunello wine** in celebration of the fall harvest.

Beyond the leaning tower, **Gioco del Ponte ("Battle of the Bridge")** in **Pisa** is a spectacular contest between the city's two rival districts, a torturous and thrilling tug-of-war tournament on the **Ponte di Mezzo** that has been played since the **16th century** by teams dressed in elaborate Renaissance armor.

Gioco del Ponte

You feel that you are experiencing more than just history as you walk through these celebrations and watch the flames of a torchlight procession flare against historic stone walls. Ancient customs are deeply embedded in even the smallest Tuscan towns, sustaining a society in which the past is not only remembered but reenacted.

CHAPTER 6: THE BEST ITINERARIES FOR EVERY TRAVELER

6.1 A Classic 3-Day Florence Itinerary: Renaissance Wonders & Local Secrets

Early in the morning, Florence's streets come alive with the scent of freshly prepared espresso emanating from the small cafés dotted throughout the old town. With the right schedule, every moment is filled with wonder, discovery, and life-altering experiences, even if it would seem impossible to entirely enjoy the city's majesty in three days. When you go into the **Duomo** in the morning, you are taken to the heart of the Renaissance, with its red-tiled dome shining against the pure blue sky.

At the starting point of the journey, **Piazza del Duomo**, the majestic **Cattedrale di Santa Maria del Fiore** commands attention. As you ascend the **463 steps** leading to **Brunelleschi's Dome** (admission includes the **Bell Tower and Baptistery**; full access costs €30), the walls engulf you in the architectural brilliance that characterized a time. The **Arno River** slashes through the city like a silver ribbon at the top, exposing Florence below in a breathtaking sea of terracotta roofs.

The **Baptistery of St. John** (€10 entry) emerges before you, its golden "**Gates of Paradise**" glittering in the early light. Inside, intricate mosaics that cover the ceiling tell biblical stories in enthralling gold. The next destination on the schedule is **Piazza della Signoria**, where the medieval-majestic **Palazzo Vecchio**, the historic seat of Medici rule, stands.

When you enter the **Uffizi Gallery** (entry €25), you are taken to a world where the Renaissance is still very much in existence. Along the walls, you'll find **Caravaggio's "Medusa," Leonardo's "Annunciation," and Botticelli's "The Birth of Venus,"** each of which tells a different story. The **Ponte Vecchio,** Florence's famed bridge, welcomes you to stroll along its fabled arches when you step outside. Once occupied by butchers and tanners, these arches now sparkle with the soft brilliance of gold jewels.

On the second day, a new rhythm that deviates from the tourist paths begins to take shape. The true Florence is in the **Oltrarno district**, which is across the river. Most visitors do not find Michelangelo's last wooden crucifix in the small, serene church of **Santo Spirito**. **Palazzo Pitti** (€16) and the sculpted beauty of the **Boboli**

Gardens (€10), where statues and fountains whisper the secrets of Medici wealth, are both within a short walk.

Santo Spirito

On the third day, the charm of the city is still evident, but there is still time for one final hidden gem. High above Florence, in a traditional ceremony, monks sing at **San Miniato al Monte**, their voices echoing through the stone walls as the city below spreads forth. It is a serene, classic moment that encapsulates the spirit of Florence's Renaissance heart.

6.2 1 Week in Tuscany: The Greatest Scenic Escape

When you leave Florence and head into the countryside, where rolling vineyards and historic towns are illuminated by golden light, the city's Renaissance glory vanishes. A week spent traveling through time in Tuscany is more than just a holiday; it's a journey where every turn leads to a story that hasn't been told yet.

Siena Cathedral

The first place you go is **Siena**, which looks to be mired in its medieval history. As you arrive, the vast, shell-shaped square of **Piazza del Campo**, teeming with history, unfolds before you. Ascending the 400 stairs of the majestic **Torre del Mangia** (€10 entry) will reward you with a breathtaking 360-degree vista of Siena's terracotta roofs that spread toward the **Chianti hills**, which are dotted with cypress trees. Inside the **Siena Cathedral** (€12 entrance), the mosaic pavement beneath your feet discloses tales of the past, while the black-and-white striped columns soar like a wonderful illusion.

The route to **San Gimignano** meanders south between olive trees and vineyards before reaching **Tuscany's most famous skyline**. Standing steadfast are the 14 stone towers of this medieval town, remnants of a time when families competed for architectural prestige. This white wine, **Vernaccia di San Gimignano** (€8 a glass) in a small enoteca, is unique to this sun-drenched hilltop town and has a crisp, refreshing flavor.

The path leads from San Gimignano into the **Val d'Orcia**, one of Tuscany's most well-known landscapes. Its rolling hills, luminous wheat fields, and lone cypress trees give the impression that it was painted during the Renaissance. In **Montepulciano**, in the heart of this valley, you may follow the scent of developing wine to **Cantina Contucci** (€20 for a guided tasting). In a 16th-century basement, the walls are covered with barrels of **Vino Nobile di Montepulciano**, their deep red colors a testament to centuries of winemaking skill.

A short drive away is **Pienza**, which offers cheese, another kind of treat. You may sample portions dripping with local honey and have a glass of **Brunello wine** (€12 for a tasting platter) **at La Taverna del Pecorino**, the home of pecorino, where the aroma of aged cheese fills the air.

La Taverna del Pecorino

On your final days, you reach **Montalcino**, a fortress-walled wine region that is among Tuscany's most renowned. The grapes at **Castello Banfi** (€50 for a lunch and gourmet wine tour) stretch on forever, producing the famous **Brunello di Montalcino**, a wine that needs to mature for at least five years before it is ready to drink. Taking place in the courtyard of a historic castle, the tasting is a unique experience that allows you to slow down time and savor the flavors of Tuscany's past, present, and future.

Cascate del Mulino

The perfect farewell as the tour comes to an end is provided by **Saturnia's natural hot springs**. Relax as the sun sets in pink and gold at **Cascate del Mulino**, a natural treasure where warm, milky-blue waters cascade over limestone terraces.

A week in Tuscany is an immersion in a way of life where elegance, tradition, and beauty coexist, and it's more than just a lovely vacation.

6.3 10-Day Ultimate Florence and Tuscany Itinerary

In a ten-day journey to Florence and Tuscany, you may experience the best of both worlds: the cultural influence of Florence's Renaissance masterpieces and the tranquil serenity of the Tuscan countryside.

Three days are devoted to discovering **Florence's** major attractions as the journey starts there. The red-bricked dome of **Brunelleschi**, an emblem of Florence's creativity, looms overhead as one passes through **Piazza del Duomo.** As you climb the 463 stairs (€30 for full access), the city below you is framed by the hills beyond. **Botticelli's ethereal Venus, Leonardo's exquisite brushstrokes**, and **Caravaggio's dramatic chiaroscuro** adorn the corridors of the **Uffizi Gallery** (€25 entry).

You can travel by rail to **Lucca**, which still has its old city walls intact and is lined with cobblestone streets that lead to hidden piazzas and **Puccini's childhood home** (entry

€10). Riding atop the ramparts, Lucca's roofs stretch out in a sea of scarlet, and the **Teatro del Giglio** can be heard in the distance, playing opera music.

Leaning Towering

Pisa is the next site, where the famed **Leaning Tower** (€18 for a visit to the top) tilts defiantly, but beyond it, there is more muted grandeur in the **Baptistery and Camposanto Cemetery.**

The air is filled with the scent of cypress trees and ripening grapes as you enter **Chianti. Castello di Brolio** (€25 wine tour) tells the narrative of Chianti Classico, from its medieval origins to the modern wines that are served on tables around the world. A local trattoria in **Greve in Chianti** delivers a **Tuscan feast** that includes truffle pasta, wild boar ragu, and a glass of ruby-red

Chianti Riserva (€45 for a complete lunch). Wineries lead to Greve in Chianti.

Castello di Brolio

San Gimignano, **Val d'Orcia, and Montalcino** are all stops along the route that contribute to the masterpiece that is Tuscany. The next few days, however, take a different route, heading toward the **Tuscan shore**. At **Castiglione della Pescaia**, along the golden dunes that stretch into the **Tyrrhenian Sea**, fishing boats bring in the day's catch, which is served fresh at a beachfront osteria (€20 for seafood pasta and wine).

Villa dei Mulini

On Elba Island, Napoleon's former residence, **Villa dei Mulini** (€5 entry), serves as a reminder of his legacy, but the island's true gem is its immaculate waters. In contrast to

Sansone Beach

Snorkeling at **Sansone Beach** lets you glide over an underwater world full of colorful fish and ancient shipwrecks, all set against the undulating hills of Tuscany. It's the perfect way to cap off a journey that allows you to experience every facet of this incredible area.

6.4 Romantic Getaway: Hidden Villages, Vineyards, and Unforgettable Sunsets

Romance in Tuscany is not found in busy cities or hurried travel schedules, but rather in the seclusion of hidden towns, the comfort of candlelight dinners, and the golden glow of vineyards at dusk.

In **Cortona**, the town that inspired Under the Tuscan Sun, time seems to slow down. Mornings begin on the **terrace of Villa di Piazzano** (€300 per night), where the rolling hills of Valdichiana stretch in every direction. You walk hand in hand through the town's old alleys, where balconies are filled with bougainvillea and windows that let in sunlight are surrounded by wooden shutters.

Bagno Vignoni is reached after a charming drive through **Val d'Orcia**. Instead of a plaza, a Roman-era hot pool shines in the middle of the hamlet. It's a refuge from the outside world, with only the gentle trickle of water over smooth stone to be heard when soaking in the nearby natural hot springs (entry €20).

When you get to **Montalcino**, you'll be greeted by the famous **Castello Banfi** (€50 for a wine tasting at dusk). In the castle courtyard, the last of the day's rays shine on glasses of **Brunello di Montalcino**. The wine's deep, rich flavors reflect the earth's history as it is aged in oak barrels and exposed to the Tuscan sun.

The final night is spent in **Florence**, the romantic hotspot of **Piazzale Michelangelo**. You grasp that **Tuscany** is more than just a destination; it is a feeling, a hug, a dream fulfilled in the warmth of its people, its land, and its timeless beauty. You hold on to the moment as the sky turns pink and the **Arno River** reflects the golden glow of the city lights.

Chapter 7: Tuscany's Outdoor Adventures Hidden Escapes

7.1 Hiking the Rolling Hills: The Most Beautiful Trails in Tuscany

As the morning sun gently glides across the Tuscan landscape, the sky is painted in soft pink and gold hues. The fresh air is filled with the earthy scent of dew-kissed vineyards and wild flora that grow unchecked along ancient roads. Hiking in Tuscany is more than simply a physical experience; it's a journey through history, nature, and a way of life that hasn't altered over the years.

One of the most beautiful routes is via the **Val d'Orcia**, a UNESCO-listed beauty of rolling hills, winding country roads, and little villages that seem to rise out of the mist at dawn. The only sound on the 14-kilometer **Pienza to Montepulciano trail** is the steady crunch of gravel beneath your feet as it winds through picturesque wheat fields and lanes lined with cypress trees. You stop at **Cappella della Madonna di Vitaleta**, a small stone church that stands alone in the vast countryside, to unwind before the day's journey begins.

Pienza to Montepulciano Trail

Chianti Wine Trail

Further north, you can follow the **Chianti Wine Trail** to discover Tuscany's famous vineyards. The scent of aged wine from oak barrels resting in chilly vaults fills the 16-kilometer trek from **Greve in Chianti to Castellina in Chianti**, which winds past rolling vineyards, historic hamlets, and hidden farmsteads. You **Castello di Verrazzano**, a famous vineyard dating back to the Renaissance, before continuing on over the countryside. There, a guided tasting tour (€30) allows you to savor the rich, velvety flavors of Chianti Classico.

Prato delle Macinaie to the Summit Route

For those seeking an experience beyond the vineyards, **Monte Amiata**, Tuscany's highest summit, offers a unique kind of beauty. The ancient volcano, which is covered in thick forests of chestnut and beech trees, may be seen from a number of trails. As you ascend the **Prato delle Macinaie to the Summit Route** (10 km), the dense canopy overhead occasionally opens to reveal panoramic views that stretch as far as Umbria and Lazio. The fresh mountain air fills your lungs.

Walking in Tuscany is more than just getting where you're going. It's about feeling the earth underfoot, the wind muttering about the past, and the sun lowering behind hills that have withstood the test of time with grace.

7.2 The Tuscan Coast: Beaches, Islands, and Seaside Escapes

The air is thick with the scent of salt as you make your way down Tuscany's **Etruscan Coast**, where golden beaches and rocky cliffs stretch out to the horizon. In contrast to the rolling vineyards and historic villages inland, the shore offers a different kind of beauty—wild, untamed, shaped by the sea and the winds. The slower pace of life here is influenced by the tides, the calls of seagulls, and the sound of the waves crashing against the shore.

Castiglione della Pescaia

You begin at **Castiglione della Pescaia**, a medieval fishing village perched on a hill overlooking the **Tyrrhenian Sea**. From the stronghold at the top of the town, you can view the golden sands of the **beaches of Roccamare and Le Rocchette** below, which are brushed by gentle waves and the immaculate waters. From the small trattorias that line the narrow streets, the scent of fish permeates the air. As they walk down to the dock, fishing boats bob rhythmically in the sea, their nets piled high with the day's catch. At **Ristorante Il Ritrovo**, a crisp glass of **Vernaccia di San Gimignano** is served with a plate of **spaghetti alle vongole** (€18), which includes clams that are still briny from the sea.

Cala Violina

Further down the coast lies **Cala Violina**, a hidden gem that is home to one of Tuscany's most pristine beaches. There are no roads that lead directly there; thus, the only way to get there is to walk **1.5 km through a protected pine forest**. The effort is rewarded when you reach the cove, where the white sand beneath your feet produces a violin-like sound. The water is extremely translucent, changing its turquoise hues with the sun. The pure beauty of nature, perfect for swimming or simply enjoying the tranquility, is all that is present here—no beach clubs or crowds of tourists.

Elba Island

From **Piombino**, you board a ferry (€20 round-trip) from the mainland to **Elba Island**, the largest and most picturesque of Tuscany's archipelago. As the boat cuts through the deep blue waters, Elba, with its rocky cliffs rising from the sea and covered in **ancient vineyards and Mediterranean scrub**, can be seen in the distance. You may visit **Napoleon's former residence** (€5 entrance) in Portoferraio, the island's historic capital, where he lived during his exile in 1814, his dreams of conquest fading into the island's peaceful, slow pace.

Monte Capanne

Sansone Beach offers an underwater world filled with marine life, with beautiful white stones leading to water so clear it appears to be glass. The beaches of Elba are diverse and pristine. **Fetovaia**, where the surrounding cliffs create a perfect, hidden harbor, is where golden sand and sapphire-blue waters meet. Hiking up **Monte Capanne** (6 km, €18 for a cable car trip to the summit) offers adventurers a breathtaking view of the entire island, with the shoreline looping around the deep blue sea.

Marina di Alberese

The **Maremma region** is reached by sailing south along the coast, where the beaches become wilder and more spectacular. The unspoiled beach at **Marina di Alberese**, which is part of the **Maremma Natural Park** (vehicle admission €10), is a stretch of white sand where wild horses wander the dunes and driftwood sculptures line the coast. Birdsong fills the pine-scented air as the waves pound the beach incessantly. There are no sun loungers or bars—just nature in its most pristine state.

As the sun begins to drop, you arrive in **Baratti**, the meeting point of Tuscany's history and the sea. Scattered throughout the golden sands, hidden just beneath the dunes, are the graves and relics of the **Etruscan civilization**. At **Populonia Archaeological Park** (€10 entry), you may discover the remains of an ancient city where soldiers sailed on wooden ships and commerce traded goods with distant locations. The water has long been a part of Tuscany's history, with its waves carrying echoes of the past.

Baratti

While dining on the terrace of **Osteria del Mare**, a seafood restaurant with a view of the Gulf of Baratti, you raise a glass of **Bolgheri Vermentino** (€7 a glass) to the horizon as the sun sets over the endlessly blue **Tyrrhenian Sea**. More than just a destination, the Tuscan coast is a sanctuary where land and water cohabit and time seems to stand still.

7.3 Hot Air Balloon Rides Over Vineyards

Hot Air Balloon

The sky is still black as you arrive at a secluded field outside **San Casciano in Val di Pesa**, a small village nestled in the center of Chianti. The chilly air has the scent of dew-soaked grass and distant vineyards. A massive fabric dome, deflated on the ground, its vibrant hues muted in the early morning light. The balloon's form expands in the early morning light as the burners flare up, filling it with hot air and gradually lifting it off the ground.

You receive a thrill of exhilaration as you get into the **wicker basket**. Everything is quiet but for the occasional burst of flame from the burner overhead. Then, silently, the ground starts to give way, and the countryside spreads up in front of you. The hills that once appeared formidable as you traveled over them now appear as soft waves of green and gold, and the vineyards and olive groves stretch out in perfect rows into the horizon.

Long shadows are cast by the rooftops of the historic structures as the town's famous towers soar above **San Gimignano**. With stone farmhouses dotted over the hills, their red-tiled roofs shining in the early morning light, and winding roads that wind through the countryside before disappearing into footpaths dotted with cypress trees, the entire valley looks like a scene from the Renaissance.

As the morning fog spreads across the valleys like a white ocean, the **Val d'Orcia** appears farther south in layers of mist. The winding road to **Monticchiello**, one of Tuscany's most beautiful villages, leads down to a set of honey-colored stone buildings on the slope. The village seems to have withstood the test of time from this angle, with stories from long ago etched on its walls.

As the sun rises higher, the **Castello di Brolio**, its stronghold guarding the nearby vineyards, comes into view. Here, **Baron Bettino Ricasoli** created the blend of **Sangiovese, Canaiolo, and Malvasia** that would eventually become one of Italy's most famous wines, Chianti Classico. From above, the vineyards appear as a patchwork of rich reds, golds, and greens, their vines bearing the promise of the next harvest.

Time seems to halt throughout the hour-long flight, which is a journey into the sky. The **Arno River** shimmers, reflecting the beautiful hues of the sky, and below, tiny villages emerge from the mist, their church bells ringing softly over the hills. The only sound to disturb the profound silence is the occasional gasp from tourists admiring the landscape from this unusual vantage point.

As the balloon begins its slow descent, a field beside **Monteriggioni**, with its historic walls forming a complete circle on the landscape, comes into view. As it lands, the basket makes slight contact with the ground before settling. Now, when you step outside, the dawn light embraces the landscape in its entirety.

The traditional Tuscan breakfast consists of freshly baked cornetti, pieces of **prosciutto crudo,** and **Pienza pecorino cheese**. It is eaten with a celebratory glass of Prosecco, whose bubbles reflect the excitement of the flight. The event, which costs around €250 per person, is more than just a luxury; it's a memory woven into Tuscany's breathtaking landscape.

You realize that the best way to appreciate Tuscany's beauty is not just on foot or by car, but to see it from above. Looking back at the sky, where the balloon is now soaring toward another horizon, makes this clear.

7.4 Thermal Baths & Natural Springs: Relaxing in Saturnia & Beyond

The journey to **Cascate del Mulino** in **Saturnia** travels through the **Maremma countryside**, where medieval towns built on hilltops and old olive groves coexist with undulating meadows. The world gets quieter the farther you travel; the busy trattorias of Siena and the thronged piazzas of Florence are gone. Here, where the countryside thrives, untouched and ageless, is one of Tuscany's most breathtaking natural wonders.

As you approach, the scent of sulfur fills the air, signaling your approach. The waterfalls, a series of blue, steaming pools that cascade down limestone terraces with their mineral-rich waters continuously flowing from far below, appear out of nowhere. Since warriors and emperors sought its healing properties throughout the **Roman era**,

Cascate del Mulino has existed as a natural bath. Unlike modern thermal resorts, this place is still completely wild and uncontrolled, and anyone who wishes to experience its warm embrace can do so.

It is a **pleasant relief** to take the first step into the water. The constant 37.5°C (99.5°F) temperature is perfect for releasing stress and letting minerals enter your skin, leaving it feeling refreshed and silky. The gentle pressure of the cascading water creates a natural hydromassage that relaxes muscles. When you close your eyes and let the sound of the falls drown out the outside world, for a brief while, all that is present is the warmth, the sound of the water flowing, and the sense of being surrounded by nature itself.

Despite its appeal, many tourists are unaware of **Cascate del Mulino** since it is frequently overshadowed by the historic cities and vineyards of **Tuscany**. But for those who find it, it's a sanctuary, a break from time itself. If you get there early, just after sunrise, you can just take in its charm. The early mist coming from the pools creates an otherworldly atmosphere. As people begin to congregate around lunchtime with picnic baskets and bottles of local wine, the encounter turns into a social ritual as old as Tuscany itself.

Terme di Saturnia Spa & Golf Resort

For those seeking a more luxurious spa experience, the **Terme di Saturnia Spa & Golf Resort** is only a short drive away. The same hot waters have been transformed into luxurious thermal pools here, complete with private soaking spaces and wellness services (day tickets cost between €30 and €50, depending on the season). While relaxing in infinity pools with views of the surrounding countryside, guests can savor herbal infusions while alternating between steam rooms, mineral baths, and mud treatments.

Beyond Saturnia: Additional Unknown Tuscan Hot Springs

There are many lesser-known hot springs in Tuscany, each with its own distinct charm and personality, even though **Saturnia** is the most well-known. An hour's drive to the north is the remote **Val d'Orcia** highlands, home to the unique town of **Bagno Vignoni**. The center of the hamlet is a vast thermal pool, where steam rises from the surface and warms the air even in the winter, in place of a normal plaza. For more than **2,000 years**, pilgrims, poets, and lords have been drawn to these waters because of their claimed healing effects. Among them were **Lorenzo de' Medici** and **Saint Catherine of Siena.**

Terme Bagno Vig

A simple stroll will lead you to the **Parco dei Mulini**, a series of free outdoor hot springs buried away in the countryside where warm water falls into natural rock basins that are suitable for a calm bath, even though the ancient piazza's pool is now only available for observation. Nearby, **Terme Bagno Vignoni** offers a more luxurious spa experience with mud treatments, massages, and thermal baths (€10 entry).

San Filippo's Fosso Bianco

One of Tuscany's most surreal views may be found north of **Siena** at **San Filippo's Fosso Bianco**. The hot springs here have sculpted the limestone cliffs into enormous, white mineral formations that seem like frozen waterfalls. As you proceed through the dense forest, you can hear the sound of flowing water more clearly until you arrive at a collection of naturally formed ponds with milky-blue waters that have been warmed by underground volcanic activity. Among these, **"The White Whale"** is the most famous. Hot water flows down the curved surface of this enormous, otherworldly rock formation, creating small bathing pools at its base.

Because of its remote location, San Filippo is remarkably tranquil even in the midst of summer. Unlike Saturnia, where the falls are always flowing, this place has hidden pools tucked away between rocks and trees, some of which are just warm enough to relax in, while others are hot enough to feel like a natural sauna.

Rapolano Terme

When you arrive in the late afternoon, when the golden light filters through the trees, you can enjoy a truly wonderful experience where the forest, river, and stream create an atmosphere of complete calm. For those looking for a more modern and luxurious spa, **Rapolano Terme**, located between Siena and Arezzo, is home to two of Tuscany's most well-known wellness centers, **Terme Antica Querciolaia and Terme San Giovanni** (€20 to €40 day passes, depending on services chosen). These spas offer hydrotherapy treatments, steam rooms, and thermal pools, fusing state-of-the-art facilities with natural mineral waters. One of the greatest spa retreats in the area, the outdoor pools, especially during the winter, offer a contrast between the crisp air and the warm, engulfing waters.

Chapter 8: The Ultimate Food Wine Experience in Florence Tuscany

8.1 Where to Find the Best Bistecca alla Fiorentina

Bistecca alla Fiorentina

The smell of grilled meat fills the streets of Florence as the fires of historic trattorias prepare to honor the city's favorite dinner. In a normal restaurant, the **Bistecca alla Fiorentina** ceremony begins with the proud presentation of the raw, marbled steak to you before it is burned. The cut, which weighs more than 1.2 kilograms and is over two inches thick, is often cooked rare or at most medium-done. Any request for a well-done steak is met with a shake of the head and a denial since a real Florentine steak is never overdone.

Trattoria Mario

Handwritten menus cover the walls of **Trattoria Mario**, and the vibe is contagious. is a place for foodies, not for formality, and the steak arrives sizzling on a platter, its charred skin encasing the delicious delicacy inside. **Regina Bistecca**, a short distance from the Duomo, offers a more polished experience. Here, a sommelier pairs each bite with a glass of **Brunello di Montalcino**, whose deep crimson undertones accentuate the steak's rich, buttery flavor. The ancient wooden tables and low lighting transform the dinner into a celebration of Tuscan heritage.

Officina della Bistecca

Officina della Bistecca, accessible via the narrow streets of **Panzano in Chianti** for a country retreat, offers a communal eating experience at the hands of **Dario**

Cecchini, Tuscany's most famous butcher. Long tables are occupied by passionate foodies who savor portions of expertly prepared steak served with crisp Tuscan bread and local olive oil. Still glistening from the fire, the meat's rich, smoky flavors convey a story of history, perseverance, and Florence's unshakable devotion to her most well-known recipe.

People are looking for the perfect **bistecca alla fiorentina** outside of the city limits. Situated in the rolling hills outside of Florence, **Ristorante Perseus** offers a view of vineyards stretching into the horizon while its steak is expertly cooked over oak flames. The setting at **I'Brindellone**, in the less well-known San Frediano area, on the other hand, is warm, rustic, and bustling with locals who are laughing because they know they are enjoying some of the best steak in the world.

With each bite, **bistecca alla Fiorentina**, a dish as bold and unforgettable as the city itself, honors Tuscany's farmers and soil.

8.2 A Exploring of Florence's Iconic Cafés and Gelato Shops

Florence rises to the perfume of freshly ground espresso beans and the sound of coffee cups clinking on marble countertops. Amidst the city's ritualistic café culture, standing at the bar with a flaky cornetto and a cappuccino is the perfect way to start the day. **Established in 1733, Caffè Gilli** has long been a meeting spot for intellectuals, writers, and artists, with chandeliers gleaming above polished wood and gilded mirrors. A well-balanced espresso (€1.50) is rich and velvety, and the first sip is a fleeting but powerful moment of pure Italian luxury.

Caffè Gilli

The journey continues outside to **Caffè Rivoire**, where the specialty is not just coffee but also the famous, rich, creamy, and nearly decadent cioccolata calda from Florence. Sitting at an outside table in **Piazza della Signoria** and watching the city's motions, the warmth of the chocolate is as calming as the timeless beauty of Florence itself.

Caffè Rivoire

Gelateria Edoardo

As the day heats up, the search for gelato begins. Each scoop of gelato is created using techniques that have been perfected over decades, making it richer, creamier, and more flavorful than ice cream. The organic, homemade gelato at **Gelateria Edoardo**, near the **Duomo**, is served in freshly baked waffle cones, and the air is filled with the perfume of sugar and vanilla. The **Crema Fiorentina**, a delicate concoction of cream, honey, and citrus zest, captures the essence of the city.

Gelateria della Passera

Across the river in the **Oltrarno district**, **Gelateria della Passera** creates mouthwatering and pleasing flavors, ranging from ricotta and fig to saffron and almond. The store is notable despite being as little and unobtrusive as the gelato itself.

Vivoli

The smoothness and richness of the dark chocolate and pistachio gelato at **Vivoli**, one of Florence's oldest gelato shops, have been enjoyed by the inhabitants for decades.

From morning coffee to late-night gelato, Florence's cafés and gelaterias provide moments of pleasure woven throughout daily life, much like the city itself.

8.3 Wine Tasting in Chianti and Montalcino: An Guide to the Best Vineyards

With each turn of the road through **Chianti Classico**, a fresh picturesque view of vineyards, old castles, and cypress-bordered estates is revealed. The rolling hills between Florence and Siena, which make up the heart of Tuscany's wine region, are home to some of the world's finest wines.

Antinori nel Chianti Classico

History and wine coexist at **Castello di Brolio**. The 800-year-old stronghold, still under the heirs of **Baron Ricasoli**, greets visitors inside its historic wine vaults, where wood barrels hold the rich, scarlet hues of **Chianti Classico Riserva** (€25 for a tour and tasting). Each sip is strong, well-structured, and imbued with the flavors of Tuscan herbs and black cherries, reflecting the region itself.

Antinori nel Chianti Classico appears to be a modern-day wine shrine as you move further into the countryside. Amid the estate's architectural marvel that disappears into the hills are modern fermentation chambers and a subterranean maturing cellar (€30 per sampling). The delicate, well-balanced wine, with its flavors of wood and wild berries, complements the region's rich cuisine.

Montalcino, further south, produces **Brunello di Montalcino**, a powerful, long-aging wine that captures the essence of Tuscany. An endless array of vines, each carefully cultivated to produce one of Italy's most prestigious wines, may be seen in the panorama at **Poggio Antico** (€35 per sample).

In the murky basements of **Fattoria dei Barbi** are bottles with yellowed labels that have aged for decades. The sommelier describes the land, climate, and maturing process that give Brunello its deep, velvety depth as he pours a **2010 vintage** (€40 per bottle).

Fattoria dei Barbi.

Every vineyard has a story to tell, and every glass of wine represents the nation and the people who have been growing it for generations.

8.4 Traditional Tuscan Dishes You Must Try

Tradition, simplicity, and the land itself are the foundations of Tuscany's tastes. Using only the freshest ingredients, centuries of inventive cuisine, and an unflinching respect for the seasons, each meal tells a story. You start to appreciate that Tuscan cooking is about letting each component shine rather than about lavishness when you sit at a rustic wooden table in a rural osteria or a Florentine trattoria.

Ribollita

You are brought a hot bowl of **ribollita**, the area's well-known bread soup, whose smell is full of cannellini beans, slow-cooked veggies, and a dusting of golden olive oil. In order to reduce food waste, this recipe was initially devised as a peasant dinner. A combination of **Tuscan kale**, carrots, and onions was used to warm stale bread, transforming simple ingredients into a hearty and incredibly tasty meal. **Trattoria Sabatino**, one of Florence's oldest family-run restaurants, serves the ribollita just as it was a century ago for just €10, but it's far more precious in flavor and tradition. It's cozy, hearty, and rich.

Pappardelle al Cinghiale

On the opposite side of the table, the waiter sets a plate of **pappardelle al cinghiale**, which are wide ribbons of homemade pasta encased in a slow-cooked wild boar ragu. This dish has strong, distinctively Tuscan qualities and comes from the region's hunting traditions. **Osteria Vini e Vecchi Sapori**, tucked away next to the **Uffizi Gallery**, offers ragu cooked for hours in **Chianti wine**, juniper, and bay leaves, as well as freshly rolled pasta every morning. At €15 per dish, the ragu melts on your tongue and has just the right amount of richness and spice.

Pici all'Aglione

In the heart of **San Gimignano**, a town known for its ancient towers and **Vernaccia white wine**, a dish of **Pici all'Aglione** is delivered to your table. This hand-rolled pasta is a thicker, more rustic version of spaghetti and is topped with a vibrant tomato and garlic sauce made with aglione, the unique, mild-flavored garlic from Tuscany. A reminder that Tuscan cooking is all about presenting the best of what the country has to give is the simplicity of this dish, which is served at **Ristorante Bel Soggiorno** and costs €12 per plate while overlooking the rolling **Val d'Elsa vineyards**.

Further south, the pungent aroma of the cheese shops that line the streets of **Pienza**, the birthplace of **Pecorino Toscano**, draws you in. Within **Marusco & Maria**

Formaggi, a local cheesemonger serves you a slice of aged **Pecorino** sprinkled with chestnut honey. The aged Pecorino's nutty, salty richness is balanced by the honey's delicate sweetness. With a glass of **Brunello di Montalcino** (€10 per sampling set), its flavor combination is so tremendously satisfying that you can immediately understand why this cheese has been a mainstay for generations.

Fettunta

The most simple yet incredibly satisfying snack, **fettunta**, is a must-have for any Tuscan dinner. A thick slice of wood-fired Tuscan bread is roasted until golden, then brushed with raw garlic, sprayed with freshly squeezed extra virgin olive oil, and sprinkled with sea salt. It shimmers in the afternoon sun as you taste the green, spicy olive oil (€5 per dish) at **Osteria del Borgo** in **Montepulciano**. Every fall, it is a celebration of the land, the trees, and the industrious farmers who mill this liquid treasure.

The server serves **cantucci**, the area's renowned almond-studded biscotti, and a little glass of **Vin Santo**, a golden-hued dessert wine, as the supper comes to a conclusion. Before biting into the biscotti, it is usual to dip it into the wine and allow it to soften. You get the sensation that time has stopped and that there is nowhere else in the world you would rather be because of the languid speed of the moment, the nutty crunch of the cookie, and the sweet, honeyed richness of the wine (€8 per serving).

Rather than producing elaborate dishes, the aim of Tuscan cooking is to enjoy the regional cuisine. Whether it's the depth of a slow-cooked ragu, the sharp bite of **Pecorino**, the warmth of a bowl of **ribollita**, or the sweetness of a biscotti dipped in wine, each meal is a chapter in Tuscany's culinary history that is ready to be enjoyed and remembered.

Chapter 9: Where to Stay: The Most Charming Places to Stay in Florence and Tuscany

9.1 Luxury Hotels: Iconic Stays and Unmatched Elegance

In cities like Tuscany and Florence, which are renowned for their timeless elegance, staying at a premium hotel offers more than just a comfortable stay; it's a chance to experience a world of magnificent history, first-rate service, and stunning beauty. Each hotel is an artistic creation designed to immerse guests in a lavish, elegant, and creative environment.

Portrait Firenze, located on the **Arno River**, offers unparalleled views. The floor-to-ceiling windows provide a stunning view of the **golden glow** of **Ponte Vecchio** at sunset, and the air is infused with the subtle scent of fresh flowers and leather. The personalized concierge service ensures that every guest enjoys **Florence** in the most luxurious way possible, whether it's a private tour of the **Uffizi Gallery**, a personalized shopping experience at **Via de' Tornabuoni, or a riverfront aperitivo** prepared on your balcony. The cost of a room ranges from €800 to

€1,500 per night, but every euro spent feels like an investment in a once-in-a-lifetime opportunity.

Portrait Firenze

Belmond Hotel

A short drive into the rolling **Chianti vineyards** is the royal retreat of **Castello di Casole**, a **Belmond Hotel** in a restored 10th-century stronghold. Every morning, a mild wind sweeps through the olive trees and cypress-lined pathways, infusing the air with the perfume of lavender and rosemary. The wine tastings in the private cellars transport you into the heart of Tuscany's richest flavors, while the infinity pool, which is set on a hill, reviews out an unbroken panorama of golden plains and valleys covered in grapes. A stay here feels like a scene from a Renaissance painting because of every tiny detail, from the antique furnishings to the comforting glow of candlelit dinners beneath the medieval arches. It is an experience that cannot be equaled in the Tuscan countryside, with costs ranging from €1,000 to €2,500 a night.

Il Salviatino

Nestled in the **tranquil hills of Florence**, **Il Salviatino** offers boutique luxury accommodations inside a Renaissance home from the **15th century**. When you wake up, the first thing you see through the arched windows is the breathtaking view of Florence's cityscape, with the **Duomo** rising like a crown over the red-tiled buildings. The Michelin-starred restaurants, the private terraced gardens, and the opulent spa treatments that use **Tuscan plants** all contribute to the elegant yet peaceful ambiance. Visitors can take in Florence's cultural diversity before retreating into the tranquility of the countryside because the city center is only fifteen minutes away. With prices starting at €750 per night, it's the perfect getaway for anyone who wants to experience the best of both worlds—artistic grandeur and rural leisure.

Rosewood Castiglion del Bosco

For visitors seeking unmatched tranquility, **Rosewood Castiglion del Bosco** in **Montalcino** offers a private estate experience within a UNESCO-listed setting. Every villa on the estate has a story to tell, with exposed stone walls, ceilings made of wooden beams, and fireplaces that have warmed hearts for centuries. Your days could be spent exploring nearby historic towns like **Pienza**, exploring **Brunello di Montalcino**-producing vineyards, or simply enjoying a private picnic with the estate's finest wines, prepared by an on-site chef. It is the ultimate in **Tuscan luxury** and a place for people seeking complete seclusion, with nightly rates ranging from €1,500 to €3,000.

Grand Hotel Continental

Last but not least, the **Grand Hotel Continental** in **Siena** transports guests to the magnificence of the Renaissance, with its superb frescoes, soaring ceilings, and antique furnishings that emit an aura of aristocratic elegance. Because of the hotel's advantageous position, travelers can easily experience the city's architectural wonders by strolling to the **Siena Cathedral** and **Piazza del Campo**. Every evening, the rooftop patio transforms into a peaceful refuge where visitors may drink aged **Chianti** while taking in the ancient skyline of **Siena's sparking lights**. Prices range from €450 to €900 per night, providing a luxury yet fairly priced choice to take in the beauty of the oldest city in Tuscany.

9.2 Low-Cost Hotels: Affordable Comfort in Prime Locations

Not every traveler to Tuscany is searching for lavish chandeliers or lobby areas lined with marble, even though comfort and authenticity are important. Thankfully, travelers on a limited budget can select charming, well-located hotels that allow them to enjoy Tuscany's highlights without going over budget.

Hotel Nizza

A short distance from the Duomo, **Hotel Nizza** in **Florence** offers cozy and affordable lodging. A day of touring is best started with the continental breakfast, which consists of freshly baked pastries and local cheeses. The warm atmosphere is created by the traditional terracotta floors and the comfortable wooden furnishings. The position is unmatched, with the **Galleria dell'Accademia, Ponte Vecchio, and Mercato Centrale** all within walking distance. With prices ranging from €90 to €150 per night, it is one of the most reasonably priced accommodations in the city.

Hotel Chiusarelli

The **Hotel Chiusarelli** in Siena effectively captures the splendor of **19th-century Tuscany** with its large, light-filled rooms, wrought-iron balconies, and a terrace that looks out over the roofs of the ancient city. Visitors may easily see the **Siena Cathedral, Torre del Mangia**, and the city's lesser-known streets thanks to its handy location just outside of Piazza del Campo. Breakfast is served on a patio surrounded by lemon trees, and the early air is filled with the soft ringing of the town's church bells. From €110 to €170 per night, it provides the ideal mix of affordability and classic grandeur.

Albergo San Martino

Inside the ancient Renaissance walls of Lucca, the **Albergo San Martino** offers guests a cozy retreat with modern amenities. The hotel's location makes it to explore Lucca's famous Gu**inigi Tower, the San Michele in Foro Church,** and the city's characteristic tree-bordered castle walls. Visitors can rent bicycles and ride along the tops of the walls for magnificent views of the distant undulating hills and homes with red tiles. With prices ranging from €80 to €140 per night, it is an excellent option for those seeking both comfort and excitement.

Hotel Bel Soggiorno

In **San Gimignano**, where antique towers dominate the skyline, the **Hotel Bel Soggiorno** provides a reasonably priced yet quaint stay. You can walk to the town's artisan gelato shops, historic wine cellars, and panoramic overlooks, and you can wake up to sweeping vistas of the nearby vineyards. It costs between €100 and €160 a night and is the best choice for people who want to experience the rustic charm of one of **Tuscany's most attractive villages.**

Hotel Bologna

Finally, the **Hotel Bologna** in **Pisa** offers a pleasant and affordable stay near the **Leaning Tower**. It offers complimentary bike rentals so you may explore the city's hidden gems, modern rooms, and a **beautiful courtyard**. The **Piazza dei Miracoli**, the **Arno River** promenade, and **Pisa's hidden botanical gardens** are all within walking distance, allowing visitors to explore the city beyond its most famous monument. With prices ranging from €90 to €150 per night, this is the ideal spot to stay for people who like to visit **Pisa** outside of the well-known tourist attractions.

Tuscany shows that budget travel doesn't have to mean sacrificing experience; it allows guests to enjoy the region's natural splendor, gain an intimate glimpse of its culture, and wake up each morning within a short distance from some of the most breathtaking locations on the planet.

9.3 Hostels: Budget-Friendly Accommodations with a Social Atmosphere

For individuals who value social contact, interesting experiences, and reasonably priced travel, Tuscany's hostels are the perfect place to start. Whether they are exploring the bustling streets of **Florence** or the medieval treasures of Siena, hostels allow backpackers, lone travelers, and thrifty explorers to stay in popular locations while mingling with other adventurers.

Plus Hostel Florence is located in the heart of **Florence** and offers one of the most lively and well-equipped hostel experiences in the city. With a rooftop terrace overlooking the **Duomo**, a swimming pool, and a bustling bar area, this hostel feels more like a chic hotel than an inexpensive place to stay. Because it's only a ten-minute walk to the **Galleria dell'Accademia**, guests may rise early and see **Michelangelo's David** before the crowds

147

arrive. After a day of exploring the **Ponte Vecchio, Uffizi Gallery, and Piazza della Signoria,** guests may enjoy Tuscan-style pizzas and local wines at the hostel's on-site restaurant. It's a great offer for anyone looking to see Florence in a lively and welcoming environment, with private rooms starting at €90 per night and dorm beds starting at €35.

Plus Hostel Florence

Ostello Bello Firenze in the **Oltrarno** neighborhood offers a cozy, rustic environment with communal meals, live music evenings, and a relaxed patio garden where guests may converse over **Chianti wine** for those seeking a more relaxed, boutique-style hostel. Only a five-minute walk from the **Palazzo Pitti,** this hostel places you in the center of Florence's artisan district. It's close to all the major sights, yet far enough from the busy tourist areas. This is a fantastic option for anyone seeking a relaxed yet social stay in **Florence's trendiest district**, with private rooms starting at €95 and dorm beds starting at €40 per night.

Ostello di Siena

Going south to **Siena**, the **Ostello di Siena**, housed inside a medieval monastery, has a unique, historic attraction. Within a short walk of **Piazza del Campo**, the location of the famous **Palio horse race**, the hostel provides an ideal location for exploring Siena's old alleyways, majestic **Gothic cathedrals**, and charming wine bars. In the communal kitchen and lounge, guests may connect over homemade pasta dishes and bottles of Vernaccia wine. With nightly prices starting at €30, it is one of the most reasonably priced accommodations in the city.

Safestay Pisa

Relax at the vibrant, modern **Safestay Pisa** hostel in Pisa, which has a large outdoor garden, after a day of touring. With the **Leaning Tower** and **Piazza dei Miracoli** just a short walk away, our hostel is a starting place for seeing not only Pisa but also nearby **Lucca** and **the Tuscan coast**. With its lively common areas, organized city tours, and on-site bar, it welcomes both independent and social guests. Dorm beds start at €28 per night, while private rooms start at €75.

Lucca Hostel

The **Lucca Hostel** offers travelers traveling to **Lucca** a peaceful, private setting in a charming historic building, tucked away inside the city's medieval Renaissance walls. Explore the city's hidden piazzas, visit the renowned **Guinigi Tower**, where oak trees grow from the rooftop, and rent bikes to explore **Lucca's well-known tree-lined walls**. With overnight rates starting at €30, it is an excellent choice for those on a tight budget who want to visit one of **Tuscany's** most underappreciated cities.

You can meet other travelers, enjoy the friendliness of Italian hospitality in a welcoming, communal environment, and fully immerse yourself in the local way of life by staying in a hostel in Tuscany, all while saving money.

151

9.4 Airbnb & Vacation Rentals: Unique Home & Local Experiences

For those who want a more private and intimate travel experience, vacation rentals like **Airbnb** provide the opportunity to live like locals, waking up in charming **Tuscan apartments**, rustic farmhouses, or even ancient towers. When you reserve a private rental, you can discover Tuscany outside of the usual hotel environment, travel at your own pace, and cook local cuisine in your own kitchen.

You may get a true taste of Florentine living at **a stunning apartment** from the **Renaissance on Via dei Serragli in Florence** (€120 per night). Its towering frescoed ceilings, old wooden beams, and large arched windows transport you back to Florence's golden past. You can walk to **Ponte Vecchio, Palazzo Pitti, and the bustling Santo Spirito square**, which is located in the **Oltrarno district**. Here, local artisans, vineyards, and hidden trattorias create a lively yet relaxed atmosphere.

A stone cottage close to **Pienza** is the perfect retreat for travelers who wish to stay in a **Tuscan farmhouse** (€150 per night). You wake up to breathtaking sunrises over the **Val d'Orcia**, rolling wheat fields, and grazing sheep, creating a scene straight out of a Renaissance painting. You can visit nearby **Montepulciano** in the afternoons, try **Pecorino cheese** at neighborhood shops, or simply relax in a private garden with a glass of **Brunello di Montalcino.**

You may spend €180 per night sleeping within one of **San Gimignano's renowned medieval watchtowers**, which offer expansive views of the surrounding vineyards, if you're searching for something truly unique. It is a once-in-a-lifetime sensation to wake up on the roofs of a town that has been stuck in time, with the Tuscan countryside extending eternally below.

In the heart of **Tuscany's wine region,** a vineyard farmhouse in **Greve in Chianti** (€160 per night) is located farther south. Breakfast is served on a bright patio backed by rows of **Sangiovese grapes** in the mornings. Days could be spent trekking across the rolling hills, touring neighboring wineries, or touring the historic **Chianti villages** of **Castellina and Radda**.

Direct access to the water and a private patio overlooking the turquoise waves of the **Tyrrhenian Sea** can be found at this beachfront property in **Castiglione della Pescaia** on the **Tuscan coast** (€200 per night). This is the perfect retreat for anyone who wants to see both the **countryside** and the pristine beaches of **Tuscany**.

Airbnb and vacation rentals in Tuscany offer more than just a place to sleep; they let you explore the region like locals do, wake up in historic homes, and enjoy the beauty of **Tuscany** at your own pace.

9.5 Campsites & Rural Retreats: Sleeping Under the Tuscan Sky

In a way that no hotel could, Tuscany's campsites and agriturismos (farm stays) provide nature lovers and adventurers an opportunity to interact with the environment. Whether you're camping under the stars, staying in a wooden hamlet surrounded by vineyards, or waking up to the scent of fresh herbs and morning mist among the rolling hills, Tuscany's rural lodgings offer a peaceful and authentic experience.

Camping Firenze

At **Camping Firenze**, which lies just outside of **Florence**, visitors may enjoy the outdoors while still being close to the city's well-known attractions (tents €25 per night, bungalows €80 per night). With modern facilities, a swimming pool, and shuttle service to Florence's historic center, the campground is ideal for anybody looking to combine urban exploration with the tranquility of the countryside.

Camping Il Poggetto

Surrounded by vineyards and olive trees, Chianti's **Camping Il Poggetto** (€30 per night for tents, €100 for wooden chalets) offers a peaceful retreat after a day of wine tasting, cycling across the hills, and exploring nearby towns like **Greve and Panzano**.

Near **San Gimignano, Agriturismo Mormoraia** (€120 per night) offers a full farm stay experience where guests can pick olives, hunt truffles, and sip house-made wines while admiring the **Tuscan countryside** at sunset.

More than just a place to stay, rural stays in **Tuscany** are an opportunity to explore the countryside, lose yourself in the natural world, and awaken to a breathtakingly beautiful world.

CHAPTER 10: PRATICAL TIPS FOR TRAVELING IN FLORENCE AND TUSCANY

10.1 Language Basics: Essential Italian Phrases for Travelers

The first thing you notice when you enter Florence is the beat of the Italian language, which mixes passionate gestures, musical emotions, and a cadence that turns every conversation into a performance. You'll quickly find that knowing a few basic Italian words may make a great difference whether you visit traditional markets, rural villages, or family-run trattorias, even though many locals who work in tourist areas speak English.

Picture yourself wandering through the bustling **Mercato Centrale**, where pecorino cheese wheels, freshly baked bread, and sun-ripened tomatoes are piled high at kiosks. **"Buongiorno! Quanto costa?"** is a simple greeting to give to a vendor. What is the price? Saying "Good morning! How much does it cost?" instantly makes you smile, in contrast to the hurried business meetings in

English. As you work harder, locals become more gregarious, sharing stories, tips, and even a few extra slices of prosciutto for free with your lunch.

"Ciao!" is said enthusiastically by the waiter at **Osteria Vini e Vecchi Sapori,** a small trattoria near **Piazza della Signoria. Pronti per mangiare?** Instead of awkwardly pointing at the menu, it feels more natural to say "**Vorrei la bistecca alla Fiorentina, per favore**" (I'd like the Florentine steak, please). A "**Prego! Torna pronto! You're welcome, and please return soon!**" is often the result of saying "Grazie, era delizioso!" to your waitress after a lovely supper (Thanks, that was great!).

A welcoming winemaker at **Fattoria di Montenasso** offers you a sampling of their renowned **Vernaccia wine** if you venture west of **Florence** to the medieval village of **San Gimignano**. Asking, rather than just nodding, "Is it possible to add a "**Posso assaggiare un bicchiere di rosso?**" A spirited conversation on the history of the vineyard, winemaking methods, and even an offer to explore the estate's underground cellars follows the question, "Can I taste a glass of red?"

Navigating the winding lanes of **Tuscany** is made easier by knowing basic instructions. If you're in **Lucca**, a quick **"Dov'è la Torre Guinigi?"** will assist you in finding the entrance to the famous **Guinigi Tower**. When you inquire, "**Where is the Guinigi Tower?**" a friendly local will usually advise you in the direction of the small street that goes to the city's most well-known viewpoint.

Knowing a few phrases isn't enough to get by; it's also important for building relationships, opening doors, and enjoying the true warmth of Italian hospitality.

10.2 Money Matters: Currency, ATMs, and Tipping Culture

A stress-free journey to Tuscany is ensured by prudent money management, which ties together the picturesque alleys of Florence, the vast vineyards of Chianti, and the charming seaside resort of **Castiglione della Pescaia**.

When you step off the train at **Santa Maria Novella Station**, your first practical concern is getting euros (€), since most of Italy is centered on cash, especially in rural towns and family-run businesses. Locating an ATM (bancomat) is easy in cities like Florence, Siena, and Pisa, where big banks like **UniCredit, Intesa Sanpaolo, and BNL** have numerous **ATMs**. However, there aren't many ATMs in rural places like **Pienza or Montefioralle**, and smaller **trattorias** or artisanal stores frequently only accept cash. Before traveling to more isolated locations, take out enough cash in Florence or Siena to avoid needless delays.

Tipping is not necessary in a modest café like **Caffè Gilli** on **Piazza della Repubblic**a, where you may enjoy an espresso (€1.50 at the bar, €4 if you're sitting outside). However, it's always polite to round up your bill with a few additional pennies. This is true for trattorias as well; at **Trattoria Mario**, a classic eatery in the **Mercato Centrale**, tipping €2 to €5 for great service shows gratitude without going crazy.

At upscale restaurants like **Enoteca Pinchiorri**, where a multi-course meal can cost over €250 per person, service is frequently not covered by the bill; hence, it is considered polite to leave a **10% tip**.

Expect to pay between €30 and €50 for each tasting session when scheduling **wine tastings in Chianti**, such as **Castello di Brolio** or **Antinori nel Chianti Classico**. Giving the sommelier a compliment and buying a bottle is a wonderful way to express gratitude for the experience, even if tipping is not necessary.

It's useful to have some small cash on hand for tipping tour guides who have direct knowledge of the rich history of **Florence's Renaissance** art or for using public facilities (which cost €1 in train stations and tourist destinations like **Piazzale Michelangelo or Piazza dei Miracoli in Pisa).**

Learning Tuscany's financial etiquette involves more than just creating a budget; it also entails enhancing the experience, ensuring that transactions proceed without hiccups, and showing appreciation for the incredible hospitality that distinguishes Italy.

10.3 Essential Travel Tips: Safety, Etiquette, and Local Customs

Traveling through Tuscany involves more than just admiring Renaissance artwork, exploring medieval towns, and sipping wine in the countryside; it also entails understanding and respecting local customs, blending in with Italian culture, and handling everyday situations with poise. The generosity of the Tuscan people is undeniable, but unwritten traditions and cultural standards could make or break your vacation.

Residents of **Florence's Piazza della Signoria** seem to move with effortless grace, exchanging warm greetings, engaging in long, expressive conversations, and embracing a slower, more thoughtful way of life. Italians see every instant of life as a time to appreciate, whether it be while talking, eating, or drinking coffee, in contrast to many other countries where multitasking or rushing through meals are normal.

You approach the counter of **Caffè Gilli**, one of Florence's oldest cafés, eager to have your first Italian espresso. When seated at a table, many guests make the mistake of expecting rapid service, not understanding that comes with an additional cost. In Italy, it is customary to stand at the bar and enjoy a short caffè (€1.50) or cappuccino (€2.50) in the morning. However, if you order a cappuccino after **11 AM**, you will be quickly identifiable as a visitor because milk-based beverages are regarded as breakfast, and residents switch to espresso or macchiato in the afternoon.

Dining manners are just as vital. Enjoy a bowl of pappardelle al cinghiale (wild boar pasta, €15) at **Osteria Vini e Vecchi Sapori,** a tiny trattoria nestled away in a quiet alley close to **Ponte Vecchio**. You notice something odd while you appreciate the delicious flavors: waiters do not automatically deliver the bill. In contrast to the US, where timely service is expected, in Italy, meals are meant to be enjoyed, and it is considered rude for a waiter to hurry you. You may find yourself sitting there for an extra hour if you don't say **"Il conto, per favore"** when you're ready to leave.

Another crucial custom is greeting people appropriately. Entering a family-run business in Lucca without saying **"Buongiorno"** (good morning) or **"Buonasera"** (good evening) is considered impolite. In smaller towns like **San Gimignano** or **Volterra**, greetings typically consist of a warm grin and a few small conversations before any business is conducted. When meeting someone for the first time, a hard handshake is suitable, but friends and acquaintances usually give each other a soft peck on both cheeks, starting from the left.

Respect for churches and other places of worship is crucial in **Tuscany**, where centuries-old cathedrals and sacred buildings still have a big influence on daily life. When at the **Duomo in Florence** or the **Cathedral in Siena**, you should cover your knees and shoulders. If you chat loudly or take distracting photos, you may get a negative look from both residents and security guards. If you include a lightweight scarf or shawl in your bag, you will always be prepared to access these gorgeous areas without any issues.

Additionally, the operation of public transit is governed by unwritten norms. As soon as you board an **ATAF bus** in Florence, you must verify your ticket; otherwise, an inspector may detect you using it and fine you up to €50. Queues are more relaxed than in **Northern Europe**, and "waiting in line" typically means making polite eye contact with others while gently making your way to the front.

Slowing down is one of the best ways to fit in and enjoy the **Tuscan way of life**. Deeper, richer experiences might result from letting yourself take in the rhythm of Italian life rather than hurrying around museums, rushing from one location to another, or expecting service to be as quick as in the US or UK.

10.4 Health & Safety: Avoiding Tourist Scams and Emergency Contacts

Like any other popular tourist destination, Tuscany is not immune to petty theft, fraud, and problems, even if it is one of the safest regions in Italy. You may travel with confidence and peace of mind if you know how to be careful, steer clear of common tourist traps, and react in an emergency.

As you stroll through Florence's **Piazza del Duomo**, the beauty of Brunelleschi's dome briefly diverts your attention. In crowded locations like this, pickpockets prey on careless tourists. Theft can be prevented by using cross-body bags with zippers, avoiding carrying valuables in backpacks, and keeping your belongings safe in crowded areas. In busy train stations like Florence's **Pisa Centrale or Santa Maria Novella**, thieves occasionally work in tandem, with one diverting attention while the other searches through pockets or bags. Risk is reduced by keeping your rucksack in front of you and paying close attention to your surroundings.

Salespeople may aggressively try to sell you "discounted" jewelry, sunglasses, or trinkets while you are admiring the **Leaning Tower of Pisa**. Many of these street vendors offer their wares for "free," but after you accept them, they demand payment. The best tactic is to forcefully walk away while politely shaking your head and saying "**No, grazie**" (No, thank you).

Groups of people may pose as **fundraisers** for a false charity at tourist-heavy piazzas like **Piazza della Signoria**, requesting that visitors sign a petition before requesting a gift. These scammers usually target unsuspecting travelers who feel guilty about turning them down. By being cautious and respectfully declining any unexpected interactions with strangers, one might avoid falling into these traps.

Rental scams are another issue, particularly in Florence, where **fake Airbnb** advertisements advertise incredibly cheap apartments in desirable neighborhoods. Make bookings exclusively through reputable sites, look at ads with several reviews, and be wary of hosts who prefer direct bank transfers over official payment methods.

Time can be saved by being aware of where to go in case of a medical emergency. The primary emergency number in Italy that connects to the fire, police, and ambulance services is **112**. **Ospedale di Santa Maria Nuova**, near the **Duomo**, is Florence's top tourist hospital. While

Ospedale Santa Chiara in **Pisa** is conveniently close to the city center and has emergency supplies, **Ospedale Santa Maria alle Scotte** in **Siena** provides comprehensive medical care.

Over-the-counter medications for mild ailments like colds and stomach issues are available at **Italian pharmacies**, or pharmacies, and their highly skilled pharmacists can offer medical advice. Pharmacies are easily identified by their **green cross sign**, and in big cities, there is always at least one open.

When driving through rural areas like **Val d'Orcia or Chianti**, it may be crucial to know the location of the nearest hospital or emergency center in case of an emergency. Small towns in farther-flung places usually have local medical clinics, while major cities like **Siena, Arezzo, and Florence** have larger hospitals.

By taking a few extra precautions, you can ensure that your holiday is as simple and enjoyable as possible, even though **Tuscany** is still one of the safest and most popular travel destinations in the world. You can focus on what really matters—enjoying the stunning scenery, fascinating history, and lively culture of this amazing region—by being aware of your surroundings, safeguarding your belongings, and being ready for any emergency.

10.5 Staying Connected: Wi-Fi, SIM Cards, and Internet in Tuscany

Staying connected while traveling through **Florence and Tuscany** can transform your trip from routine to flawless, whether you need translation apps to help you in a **small trattoria in Montepulciano**, **Google Maps** to help you navigate the cobbled streets of Siena, or immediate access to travel updates while visiting remote vineyards in **Chianti**. Reliable internet connectivity enables easy reservations, seamless communication, and real-time sharing of your Tuscan experiences.

You enter **Florence's Piazza della Repubblica** and observe a tourist desperately trying to connect to public **Wi-Fi** outside a café. With the right preparation, this irritating circumstance can be completely avoided. In Tuscany, there are a number of ways to stay connected, such as using local **SIM cards** and **eSIMs**, pocket **Wi-Fi**, and reliable public hotspots.

Piazzale Michelangelo, Santa Maria Novella Station, and **Piazza del Duomo** are among the well-known locations in **Florence** where guests can connect to public Wi-Fi networks like **Firenze WiFi**. However, these networks sometimes demand registration, offer limited speeds, and might be unreliable in congested areas. Getting a prepaid **SIM card or an eSIM** before you are there is the simplest way to ensure constant connectivity instead of relying on spotty connections in tourist-heavy areas.

At **Florence Airport (Peretola)** and **Pisa International Airport**, telecom companies such as **TIM, Vodafone, and WINDTRE** offer booths where you may purchase a local SIM card with data rates starting at €20 for 10GB. If you want unlimited data, Vodafone offers a €30 bundle that allows for seamless video calls, streaming, and navigation. Purchasing an **Italian eSIM online** before a trip allows for quick activation upon arrival, saving travelers with **eSIM-capable phones** from having to swap out traditional **SIM cards**.

From the rolling hills of **Val d'Orcia** to the remote towns of **San Miniato**, traversing the Tuscan countryside necessitates visiting locations with less widespread Wi-Fi. Although rural access can be patchy, especially in valleys covered in vines or old stone buildings, hotels and agriturismos often provide **free Wi-Fi**. Even in remote locations, strong, private internet connectivity can be guaranteed by hiring a pocket Wi-Fi device, which rental shops in **Florence and Pisa** sell for around €8 per day.

Friendly cafés like **Ditta Artigianale** in Florence or **Caffè Poliziano** in **Montepulciano** have easy access to **Wi-Fi,** making them perfect places to check emails, plan trips, or share travel-related experiences. However, as laptop use is discouraged in some traditional Italian café culture, it's always a good idea to find out if extended visits for work or study are allowed.

Train stations in **Tuscany**, such as **Santa Maria Novella** in **Florence** and the main **railway hub** in **Siena**, also offer free Wi-Fi; however, the speed may vary based on the time of day. On trains, **Wi-Fi is available**, particularly on high-speed routes that connect **Milan**, **Florence, and Rome**. This allows you to enjoy the stunning scenery from your window seat while remaining connected.

For those who rely on international roaming, major European carriers such as **Orange, Three, and Deutsche Telekom** offer affordable roaming services throughout Italy. However, travelers from outside the **EU** should use caution because international roaming costs might be costly. By checking with your provider before you leave or by purchasing a travel **SIM card** designed specifically for Italy, you can prevent unforeseen expenses.

Whether you're working remotely from a Tuscan villa, exploring the alleys of **Florence's Renaissance, or video-calling** family members from a sun-drenched vineyard, being connected in **Tuscany** is easy and accessible with the right tools. By planning ahead, you can appreciate the beauty of your surroundings rather than deal with the frustration of lost connections or unplanned service disruptions.

Click on the link for a Google map of Florence and Tuscany

https://www.google.com/maps/place/Tuscany,+Italy/@4 3.3248315,8.3893458,7z/data=!3m1!4b1!4m6!3m5!1s0 x12d42b531080347b:0xbac6c3ba5b2059ab!8m2!3d43.5 671153!4d10.9807003!16zL20vMDdrZzM?entry=ttu&g _ep=EgoyMDI1MDQxNi4xIKXMDSoASAFQAw%3D %3D

Scan the QR code for a Google map of Florence and Tuscany

Made in United States
Cleveland, OH
05 July 2025

18255369R10094